PORTABLE PRAIRIE

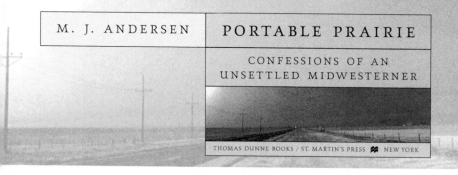

M. J. ANDERSEN

PORTABLE PRAIRIE

CONFESSIONS OF AN
UNSETTLED MIDWESTERNER

THOMAS DUNNE BOOKS / ST. MARTIN'S PRESS ☒ NEW YORK

THOMAS DUNNE BOOKS.
An imprint of St. Martin's Press.

www.stmartins.com

Book design by Jonathan Bennett

ISBN 0-312-32689-0
EAN 978-0312-32689-0

First Edition: January 2005

10 9 8 7 6 5 4 3 2 1

For my parents, who never left

CONTENTS

PREFACE

This is a story about leaving home and trying to find it again. I have made it as true to my experience as I could, which is to say it is full of contradictions and loose ends. Anyone who tells you her life is like a book has either been reading some bad books or is not being straight with you or herself about her life.

Although I no longer live there, my story is rooted in the Midwest, which has long been the imaginary home of all Americans. You are picturing it right now—a little town with a Main Street; on the edge of that town, a peaceful farmhouse surrounded by corn; pure unadulterated heartland. We leave such places precisely because we are Americans, ambitious to become something or, failing that, to have. Also, precisely because we are Americans, and steeped in the mythology of Oz, it eventually turns out that all we ever really wanted to do was go home. But this is far from the simple idea it sounds like.

In what follows, I have changed the names of people who are not close relatives and altered some details about them. And since to me, towns are like people, and similarly deserving of privacy, I have changed the names of towns as well. The eminent agriculturalist Niels Ebbesen Hansen plays himself, as do Ethel T. Wead Mick and Leo Tolstoy.

PORTABLE PRAIRIE

ASTAPOVO STATION

WE LIVE near the train tracks. They run along an embankment, just beyond a row of houses that rattle whenever a train passes by. The houses are old, but most are well kept. The one that is mint green has a narrow strip of yard on one side, and in late summer it bursts with red dahlias that look, from a distance, like roses.

These houses are just down the block from ours. From the rear bedroom on the second floor, the trains appear to whiz past at eye level. One day, one of them struck a young woman as she stood on the tracks. Some people believe that she wanted it that way. The engineer, unable to stop, knowing it would be too late, put all his strength into braking just the same. The train carried the young woman's body for several feet.

High school boys in enormous shorts, their caps turned backward, watched from the nearest bridge as the police took measurements. If it were not for the row of houses, and the trees just behind them, I could have watched the whole thing from our window—could have seen precisely where the young woman was struck, and how far the train carried her.

. . .

The local newspaper told us the young woman had been due to leave home for a new job, in upstate New York I think it was. Perhaps it was a promotion, with new responsibilities. People said the young woman had everything ahead of her, that they could not understand why she chose death, which comes soon enough.

Perhaps, on the verge of leaving, she could not see the point. She may have envisioned all the stages of life before her, a series of predictable crises and transformations, and wondered about the use of going through them. Everything would bear her farther away from home—from a native landscape fastened to the earth by train tracks and blazing maples; from the school rooms and church of her childhood.

Why should she endure this?

In the same week that adorers of Princess Diana were laying down fields of flowers in her memory (thousands of blossoms left at palace gates, the doors of embassies, places where the blond goddess might have lunched) our young woman received precisely two bouquets. They were attached to the bridge and made of common greenhouse flowers. Nobody touched them for many days. Very soon the flowers wilted and the ribbons faded. At some point, the bouquets were taken down, and the train tracks simply led to Boston again.

Leo Tolstoy is said to have written his great novel *Anna Karenina* after reading a newspaper story about a woman who threw herself in front of a train. The novel is a mountain of gorgeous detail, hundreds of pages of Anna, her husband, her lover, and all the people they knew, all of it funneling toward the moment when

Anna is standing by the tracks and understands that her choice will be death.

But Anna's choice is only the penultimate section of the book. Afterward comes the religious conversion experience of Levin. Something mystical happens to him while his wife is giving birth to their child. He understands that he must live for God, and embrace goodness. But he also understands that the moment of revelation will fall away, and that his life from this point on will not be easy. In fact, it will seem much the same. But there will be no turning back from his vision. He must repeatedly choose God.

Levin is Tolstoy's jumping-off point. After conceiving him, he must become him. He must exchange a life of art—the least doctrinaire state possible—for a life of certitude. Or so it seems.

The facts of Tolstoy's life are well known. He was born into Russian nobility and hence a life of privilege. After an interval of youthful adventure, he inherited Yasnaya Polyana, the estate about one hundred miles south of Moscow where he grew up and to which he returned after marrying. At Yasnaya Polyana, Tolstoy scribbled and studied and begat children, while serfs brought in the harvest and cared for the horses.

There is no writer alive who has not pictured Tolstoy in his study: It is crammed with books and pictures, sumptuously carpeted and finely draped. A robust fire burns in the grate while Tolstoy drafts another chapter of *War and Peace* or sits exclaiming over Schopenhauer like an excited undergraduate. (He cannot understand for the life of him why everybody is not reading Schopenhauer.)

The main thing every writer knows about Tolstoy is that he had it made: He was living the perfect writer's life at Yasnaya Polyana.

He had no teaching commitments, no deadlines he did not set for himself. He had no job as a waiter or a night watchman. He had a young wife, children, plenty of all that he needed. He even had fame. What a setup, every writer since Tolstoy has thought. What a deal.

Because he was a child there, Tolstoy must have known every inch of Yasnaya Polyana: where the snow piled highest in winter or melted first in spring; which woods offered the best hunting; which hill the finest prospect. He would have absorbed the sky in all its moods, especially the sad twilight of summer, which seemed to tell every Russian nobleman: We cannot go on this way, cannot go on with our golden samovars and silk dressing gowns, with our armies of serfs.

In the early 1880s, a few years after completing *Anna Karenina,* Tolstoy wrote *A Confession.* The book described his spiritual despair and a conversion not unlike Levin's. In the prime of his life, Tolstoy renounced his two great masterpieces and instead recommended, as the highest example of moral art, *Uncle Tom's Cabin.*

Thereafter, Tolstoy promoted a Christianity stripped to its ethical teachings, including a de-emphasis on material things. Family members and friends were appalled. They loved Yasnaya Polyana and its comforts. They wanted to keep things the same.

The worst part was that Tolstoy was attracting followers. They came to the estate on pilgrimages. One, Vladimir Chertkov, installed himself there. Chertkov was a former horse guard officer who believed in a new kind of community. Soon, Chertkov and Tolstoy's wife, the countess Sofya, were locked in a battle for Tolstoy's soul. It went on for years, until, unable to bear the tension any longer, Tolstoy fled Yasnaya Polyana.

Where was he to go? He hardly knew himself. But his end is

now famous. Tolstoy came to the train station at the village of Astapovo and died there. In one view, this is the end, duly recorded, of a great author. In another, it is an old man's confused flight from home, in a last-ditch attempt to find that very thing.

Like a number of New England mill towns, Eastboro, where I live, has a passed-over quality. The enormous Victorians erected during the town's heyday as a manufacturing capital have been divided into offices for lawyers or CPAs. The less lucky ones have been stripped of their ornamentation and entombed in vinyl siding, then carved into rental units. A few have been restored but not in the self-conscious way signifying a community's discovery of itself as "historic." What has been going on in Eastboro is something closer to maintenance.

Though relatively modest in scale, our house is one of these old Victorians. Except for its lack of a fireplace, it is exactly what I wanted. It is a big, sweet cookie of a house, pale gray, almost ridiculously archetypal with its white picket fence, farmer's porch, and white trim swagging the windows and doors like icing. In spring, pink rose and bridal wreath bushes swell with blossoms. In the fall, I deck the yard with crimson and orange mums.

In one of those maudlin moments I only get when I am alone in the car, I almost cried the first time I drove home to our house in snow. It was evening; the lights were on; the snow heaved in fine gusts around the house, which appeared suspended in the storm like a lantern.

"Our house," I thought. *"Ours."*

We had barely been there a month. The next day my husband and I shoveled what at last was our own walk. We did not mind the cold or the heavy weight of the snow. Inside, we loved the white kitchen with its neat pantry shelves; the polished floors and bull's-eye molding; the clawfoot bathtub, perfectly situated next to a small radiator; and the soapstone sink in the basement.

For a good six months, more, we went stupidly from room to room, saying: I can't believe this is our house. We looked at each other, shook our heads. It was as though the previous owners, now good neighbors, had simply given it to us, after repairing, decorating, and polishing every inch; after loving the house so fiercely themselves it seemed that nothing bad could ever happen in it.

They and other neighbors told us about everyone who had lived there before: good, happy people who had treated the house with care. There was the woman who planted the spirea bushes and never got to enjoy them in their maturity. There was the reserved bookkeeper who was utterly changed by a stroke. Before the stroke, he was a formal man who always wore a hat. Every day he walked across the bridge over the train tracks to his job in the factory and back again. After the stroke he loosened up. He told jokes, forgot to shave. His wife reportedly preferred the first version. Later, and just before us, came Bill, a born scavenger who was Jeffersonian in his zeal for improvements. He had laid out brick walkways; papered every room; constructed a greenhouse for his wife. After four years, no project remained. The melancholy of completion drove them down the block to a bigger place.

So many rooms!, Andrew and I marveled. So much cupboard space. Lights wherever you imagine you might need one. And in the spring, we would soon find, lilac and mock orange.

The house was a shared love but also, for me, a deeply personal one. I had been making my way toward this house, my first, for years. The day I signed the papers, I was only a few months shy of forty. Home, to me, was a house. But I had not lived in one since leaving for college at eighteen. All this time, it seemed to me, I had wandered in the wilderness, at best camped out. And now, I believed, that time was over.

A year before we found the house, my husband and I took a trip. We drove from our apartment in Providence to my childhood home, in South Dakota. The house in which I grew up belonged to my grandmother, who had died a few years before. Now it was to be sold, but before that happened, I had permission to remove a stained-glass window from the garage.

The window was a lozenge of pale greens and burnt sienna depicting bamboo. Before I was born, it had enjoyed a prominent place in the dining room. It was banished to the garage after picture windows became what every family wanted. The stained-glass window was placed in a wall facing the neighbors, there from my earliest days until my graduation from high school. A piece of clear glass covered the corner that had been shattered by a baseball, courtesy of my brother's friend Bruce.

It was Tom Acker who dislodged the window for us; he is a farmer whose avocation is carpentry. For a few years, during junior high, I was good friends with his daughter Janet. She knew a lot of beauty tips, and when I visited their farm, she went to work on me, teaching me how to do a steam facial over the bathroom sink. It involved a lot of cold cream and an almost unendurable interval of breathing hot, moist air with a towel tented over my head.

Janet read teen magazines. She could do her hair in perfect ringlets, apply mascara with no clumps, and execute a full manicure, complete with cuticle softening and layers of polish. I was with Janet in her basement, working on toenails, when her mother flew down the stairs one day to say Robert Kennedy had died. We took in her horror and amazement, and I remembered how the

Ackers were Democrats, which we were not, and so that made it worse for Janet's mom.

Who would be next? Mrs. Acker wondered. First the president, then Martin Luther King, now this. She could not think, did not know what to do with herself.

Her anguish seemed to me like a puzzle to figure out, a kind of math problem. For some reason, people in the world beyond our state were not behaving. Where I lived, everyone acted normal; beyond, they did not. Robert Kennedy had been killed, it sounded like, in a kitchen by a busboy. And yet it did not change the fact that our job that summer was skin care, that we needed to know about and idolize the long-haired boys in the teen magazines. They were pop music and TV stars. They sang "Hey, little woman!" and related lyrics about getting girls to cross over from childhood. It was vaguely menacing: These teen idols meant us no good. But Janet embraced the whole thing. She could not wait to be a woman and get off the farm. By the time I came home to get the stained-glass window, Janet had long ago packed up her beauty secrets and moved far away.

Andrew and I wrapped the window in a blanket and put it in the back seat. We took it through Minnesota, Wisconsin, Illinois, Indiana, Michigan. It sat waiting while some smiling French Canadians took our picture in front of Niagara Falls. It rode with us past Buffalo and Albany and Worcester to Rhode Island, where it sat in the basement of our apartment building until we found the house we knew, within minutes, we would buy.

When we moved in, we identified one or two places where the window could conceivably go. But I delayed. For weeks my fragment of home sat propped against a wall in the dining room. One day I lay on the living room couch, staring into the dining room at the window. Why could I not make the decision to install it? Several morose minutes passed before an unwanted thought came, almost as though filtering, after some trouble, through the window's pale green surface: Perhaps my yearning for a house had all along been a wish not to be home but to *go* home, back to the prairie, to live.

I could not have been more stunned if a messenger had come to the door to say I was adopted. *This* was the conclusion of my search? The whole point of the stained-glass window was that it was a delightful disguise. In my book, the fake exoticism of faux bamboo existed expressly to soften the most severe yet ravishing and unadorned landscape on earth. Bereft of that function, it became merely a pretty object in need, still, of a minor repair to its corner.

I had tried to transplant home. And I had failed. I thought of the years of saving money; of all the houses we had seen and rejected; of the effort and fear that had gone into inspections and financing; of the physical toil of yet another move. What was missing from my new home was a view of vacant land spreading for miles beyond my backyard, a view of fields and lordly skies. I lay there and was quiet for a long time. Soon after, I moved the window to the basement.

Plainville, South Dakota, was an ordinary prairie town of about thirty-five hundred people. The train station was at one end of Main Street, and the county courthouse (something our forebears fought hard to get) stood at the other. In front of the courthouse was a monument of a Civil War soldier. Like anyone who grows up in a small Midwestern town and then leaves, I can in any place and at any time close my eyes and picture the exact configuration of Main Street: on one side, the Chateau theater, Dakota State Bank, JC Penney's, the Lakota Café, the shoe store, Stemsrud's dime store. Then came Schott's bakery, with its thick sweet-greasy air; Rose Jewelry, where Grandma studied the china patterns for new brides; the Sears mail-order store.

At the end of the line, just before the train station, stood the Firestone store, redolent of virgin rubber. Along with tires, it had a baffling inventory of things I associated with men. Most of the year I took little interest. But just before Christmas the Firestone store was full of toys and open, of all rare things, into the evening. After much begging from me and my older brother, Charlie, Dad would take us downtown one night to see. We gazed at displays of model trains, at tables and shelves loaded with dolls, farm sets, army men, stuffed animals, and games. Snow melted from our boots as we moved like solemn pilgrims up and down every aisle. Our wool scarves were damp where they had covered our mouths. We turned rosy in the warmth of the store, went nuts with desire. My yearning blended with the smell of new rubber. Today I cannot ever smell new rubber without feeling a surge of well-being and pleasure. It is the pleasure of anticipating but also the pleasure of profound orientation: I have gotten my bearings. I know, somehow, where I am, in a deep sense unrelated to geography.

Charlie and I were fortunate children. We had indulgent parents and an even more indulgent grandmother. We got what we wanted for Christmas. Perhaps as a result, my idea of God expanded in unsound ways. I came to believe that prayers were generally answered and that goodness brought tangible rewards. At the same time I was taught that it was bad to want the things of the world. In the long run they would fail to satisfy. Very young, I learned to play games with my desire. I would send it out through a little gate, then wad my spirit into a ball of self-abnegation. Once I was convinced I was beyond wanting, I would open the gate again. Getting and not getting were all the same to me.

In all of the churches in our town, the soul was instructed to find its home in Jesus. First, you had to let Jesus into your heart. You had to accept him as your personal savior. He stood at the door and knocked, as though you were a little house. We saw pictures of this in Sunday school: Jesus standing at the door, knocking.

I listened to these ideas earnestly, pulled them in, and at the age of nine, during Lent, chose. I was rock-certain. Only, bypassing Jesus, I made a private deal directly with God. I then vowed to remember that this was big, that it happened at the age of nine. And indeed I have remembered. I was like Tolstoy's Levin: I would be God's from this moment on. I considered myself saved.

Our church, the Congregational, was one of the smallest in town. We were outnumbered by Catholics, Lutherans, Methodists— just about everybody. We followed a comparatively liberal theology that saw love as the point and the idea of Satan as an excuse.

Sunday school took place in the basement, on metal folding chairs set up on two sides of a short aisle. Mrs. Kallstrom read a lesson. Mrs. Voss accompanied us on a hymn. The piano was tinnysounding with big loose keys. We sang "For the Beauty of the Earth" or "The Church in the Wildwood." After our small service, we broke up into classes and sat at long tables, going over the Ten Commandments, coloring Joseph's coat of many colors, or gluing cotton onto cutouts of sheep.

In my memory, these things always took place in winter. Shortly before we arrived, women had come in to turn on the heat. The idea was to make sure that it would be warm upstairs, in the sanctuary, for the service an hour later. But in the Sunday school we were all cold. I see myself in a dress made of some thin material, and the metal folding chair is cold against my thighs. I am trying to make a tent, a small house, out of my Sunday dress.

All over the basement were pictures of Jesus. Some showed him in pastels: cream, blue, and rose. In others, his face and hair were warm browns. Jesus was tan, his robes tinged with green and gold. He was mild-looking with placid brown eyes, as beautiful as a woman. His golden brown hair fell in delicious waves that made me think of gravy.

Sunday school was followed by another hour in church. Midway through, my stomach would be completely empty, contracting with a fierce hunger that made it seem I could swallow a pew whole. Too young to take communion, I gazed at the morsels of bread heaped high in brass salvers and passed from adult to adult. I burned with my forbidden wish for just one cube of consecrated bread.

Time did not pass in church. It grew becalmed. Here was one more hymn or Bible verse or announcement or prayer. *A whole hour of this.* I would think of the roast my mother had left cooking in an electric frying pan, along with potatoes and carrots, and of the rich gravy she would make at the very end, after we got home, and which would smother everything. Christ's love smothered everything and filled you. That was our belief. We had a home in heaven, and until then we had Jesus.

The world was two worlds, divided into country kids, who lived on farms, and town kids. Mine was a town family, with a business on Main Street. Most of the time, our concerns extended no farther than the Firestone store. Other people in town felt differently. The Hamm family regularly drove down to the end of Main Street to sit and watch the trains go by. The Hamms had more children than I could ever keep count of and took as many of them on these trips as could fit inside their beat-up station wagon.

Charlie and I and our friends laughed about it. We may have lived in a hick town, but we knew what a true hick was. The Hamms' routine was pure Podunk.

Dad did not like it when we laughed. He said the Hamms did not have a lot of cash to throw around. They could not buy all those children every little thing. The movie cost a lot for a family that size, whereas the train came by for free.

It was not until years later that I found out our parents, in their early twenties with two babies, only bought gas for the car on an occasional Sunday. They would take us for a ride, driving out a little ways from town, past golden fields, past black Aberdeen Angus chewing and staring. We would drive toward the horizon, getting a big dose of sky, turn around, and come home again. That town, where we four began, was even smaller than Plainville. There was no train.

The Hamms were on something more than a cheap date. When they sat and watched the boxcars go by—car after car filled with grain—they enlarged their view of the world. Somewhere out there, in places we could barely picture, masses of people needed what we had. The rails led to great cities, to multitudes who had all kinds of different ideas on how to live. The rails also moved into the future, toward jobs no one could imagine, ingenious inventions, miraculous cures. There would be new ways of getting rich, more wealth for more of us. You only had to give your solid Midwestern kids a good start.

The Hamms, with unshakable faith, sat crowded together in

their car, in every season and every type of weather, and waited for the train. And when it came, they watched with a wonder that was the only valid response.

Though we were less conscious of it, the rails also led into the past. Prairie towns were uncertain ventures; they sprouted by the dozens during the settlement days of the nineteenth century, and every one of them aspired to be the next great American metropolis. The towns squabbled fiercely over each thing, great or small, that might give them an edge. Most important was the railroad: If the train did not come through, a town had no hope. Without the train, it was doomed to die.

By the time I was born, in the mid-1950s, the national highway system and the trucking business had begun to mount a serious challenge to the trains. Greyhound or Jackrabbit buses carried people across the farmlands to see their relatives. The buses came through town more often than the train and stopped in more places. Freight trains continued their runs. But we had only one passenger train, part of the Milwaukee Road system. It came in from Aberdeen, South Dakota, to our west, then angled northeast to Minneapolis, the greatest city in the world.

My mother loved this train with a love that made the Hamms look like mere disinterested bystanders. All year long she squirreled away quarters and spare dollar bills so that in December we could ride the train to Minneapolis, see the Christmas displays, and shop. These trips were for women and children: Sometimes our grandmother would come along but never our father. When Dad went to a place, he meant to get there on his own.

Because the train came through late at night, we laid out our clothes before bed, and slept fitfully. Mom would wake everyone sometime after midnight. Who wanted to go then? Yet we rose from our warm covers to prepare, our stomachs burning with the distress of interrupted sleep. We trembled a bit from nervousness, too, as though we faced an audition.

Having dressed and double-checked our money, we drove downtown, with not enough time for the car to warm. The angle parking spaces on Main Street were deserted. It appeared that every inhabitant of the town and perhaps the world had fled. A few neon signs were still lit, but most storefronts were dark. I had a sense of trespassing.

The station house was open, lighted, and warm but unmanned. Mom was the sort to leave herself plenty of time, yet each time it seemed possible, once we were in the station, to have missed the train. It seemed a huge error, as unbearable as forgetting to live your life.

At last, though, we detected the faint rattle of the approaching engine. "I hear it," Charlie said. We rose from our benches. We were dressed in our best clothes, our good winter coats, outfits that never looked stylish once we reached the city, no matter how hard we had tried.

The horn of the diesel engine sounded with a luxuriant, low-timbred blast, like someone warming up on a bari-sax. Then the train bore in, slowing, snorting, a complex mechanical angel that had come for us alone. We were ready to cast off all that we had and follow. If the train had taken us to meet our maker right then, we would not have dared to object. We were as ready for God as we would ever be. We were leaving our town just as it was, slumbering in the expectant hush of Advent. I felt a brief surge of envy for the children staying behind, for how they would rise in the morning to a normal day—to Saturday, the week's lustrous pearl. Ahead of us lay all the discomfort and strangeness of a journey, that thing we do to ourselves simply because it is necessary to go and see, and because no one, not even the Hamms, is ever fully reconciled to home.

For a few years in the late nineteenth century, L. Frank Baum, creator of *The Wonderful Wizard of Oz,* lived in Aberdeen, the big and important town from which the passenger train came to us. He basically bombed there, first as the operator of a dry-goods store (Baum's Bazaar), then as the editor of *The Aberdeen Saturday Pioneer,* a weekly he ran into the ground in approximately one year. After that, he fled to Chicago. His most famous book came to him about a decade later, when he was well out of the prairie.

I have long felt mixed about Baum's decision to set his story in Kansas rather than South Dakota, the prairie land I believe he actually referred to in his mind. He may have had symbolic reasons for choosing Kansas or even logical ones: Historically, Kansas has endured more tornadoes than South Dakota, including a rather large one that killed thirty-one people in two towns in 1893, not long after Baum moved to Chicago.

But I suspect the main concern was politeness. If, in a small Dakota town, you suggest that your community is not all that it could be, that a person might yearn for distant places and other types of experience, you are in big trouble. And no one understands this better than the local newspaper editor. Most of the big stories in a small Midwestern town never get printed. At best, they are only alluded to. Feelings can so easily be hurt.* You get the details on Main Street or when friends come over for a piece

---

* Subscriptions canceled.

of pie. (Pie, when I was growing up, was as vital a component of our information system as the telephone receiver.) Big media from places Out East and elsewhere, but mainly from Out East, are routinely criticized for being so critical, even by the small-town press. And do not even bring up the ACLU.

As I saw it, the forced good cheer and unrelenting boosterism of Midwestern towns had a common root. Both went back to the days when towns, still in their fledgling stage, competed for ascendancy. What railroad would ever stop for a place that was not sure of itself, a place whose own people put it down? What enterprise would arrive? What human dynamos could be tempted to settle in?

So there we all were, generations later, after all the track had been laid, with frozen smiles on our faces. We were bound to declare that everything was A-OK in our book: We did not need to have heard of Voltaire to say that this was the best of all possible worlds. What began as necessity became habit. Anybody who got too negative was a source of suspicion, if not downright alarm: This person was at least an atheist, maybe even a traitor to our country.

Baum, I suspect, knew all this; leaving may have been a relief. Mainly, it put him on the road to epic thoughts.

In *The Odyssey,* the Western world's great template for the journey away from home and back, the Greek hero Odysseus sets sail and meets many tests of his physical and mental capacities. The model is heroic. Dorothy's odyssey in *The Wonderful Wizard of Oz* is, by comparison, a cakewalk. Courtesy of a dream, she finds herself in an enchanted land. Her task is simply to get home. The tests come mainly for her companions: the Scarecrow, the Tin Man, and the Cowardly Lion. As we know from the 1939 MGM movie version of the tale, Dorothy's ultimate discovery is that there is no finer place in the world than her own backyard—than the farm in Kansas, U.S.A., where she belongs and, most important, is loved.

For decades, millions of Americans of all ages have gone misty-eyed over this discovery, and embraced it as one of the deepest truths they can know. Why is this? Why do Americans melt over the idea of going home? And why do we respond to what is essentially an act of remembering—remembering a forgotten or hidden truth—more than to an act of heroism?

Do we believe more in a God who hides from us than one who would test us? Philosophers and writers from Plato on have suggested that we are thrown into the world from some eternal realm we would immediately recognize as home. We may have forgotten it. But occasionally something in the world hints at this true home's presence. Our forgotten home is inscribed in our souls, alluded to hundreds of times in a single life—for instance, the moment the piano teacher first guides our small fingers to middle C.

However it may be, such abstractions were far from our thoughts when Charlie and I, along with most children in town, first encountered the classic film *The Wizard of Oz*. It was offered on TV once per agonizing year. In the early days we often discussed what it would be like to see the part that we knew was in color actually *in color*. Our televisions were black and white, fine for the opening scenes, which take place on the farm. But when the tornado sets Dorothy's house down in Oz, where everything in the movie version is in glorious color, Plainville's version continued in dreary black and white. The movie, of course, returns to black and white at the end. Dorothy is back home, waking up from her beautiful dream, teaching us all that black and white is just fine, as long as you are surrounded by the people you love and violins are playing.

One person who did not buy it was Grandma. If she was not the first person in town to get a color TV (probably the honors fell to one of the bankers), she came very close. Certainly she was the first in our neighborhood. We lived with Grandma in an apartment over the garage that was reached by entering her house. Thus Charlie and I were free to watch the new TV, a Zenith of piglike proportions on tiny splayed legs, situated just downstairs. The TV's smooth wooden top was like a table that could have accommodated four, which was what our family would have been without the complication of Grandma.

The Zenith was a wonder, even when there was no picture. Its "snow," when nothing was on, was like a welter of jewels, bits of blue, red, and green. Soon after it arrived in Grandma's living room, Charlie and I crept down to see our first Saturday morning cartoons in living color. We were up way too early and watched the colored snow for a long time. Finally we got Hector Heathcote, a colonial character dressed in blue, with brick-colored hair. We were transfixed, absorbing the color as though it were a long-absent basic food group.

The next time *The Wizard of Oz* rolled around, we were ready to see how the myth of home truly was: its beckoning brick road in yellow; the green costumes and horses of the Emerald City; and Dorothy in colors reprising Hector Heathcote: her blue dress, her hair a beautiful auburn. And then there was the most famous color of all: the ruby slippers, a pair of glittering red pumps that to me looked all wrong with those ankle socks Dorothy wore. And yet, *what color*! Surely we were in paradise.

The train that came to us from Frank Baum's town pulled into Minneapolis at around seven in the morning. The ritual of arrival began with watching dawn gain conviction as we entered the outskirts of the city. We glided past its poorer housing: shabby brick apartment buildings and sagging wood tenements. Scarcely breathing, my mind moving against a new sensation the way the tongue goes to a loose tooth, I stared. As I pressed my face to the thick glass, it seemed to me that it would be unbearable to live in one of these places. There were scarcely any trees. Here and there were a broken window, graffiti, trash, something boarded up. Everything was crowded together, home piled upon home.

I felt the kind of guilt masked as irritation that is common to those whose wants are answered. Why didn't they work harder, I wondered—the great and numberless "they" out there? At the same time, I sensed that I could not know the barriers to an orderly existence in such places. Why had God permitted such an awful life (for surely it was awful here)? The God I had heard about was loving, not punishing. So what was the big idea here, on the outskirts of Minneapolis, Minnesota—on the way to stores so full of fine things no one could take in more than a fraction of it all?

I would imagine becoming lost in the city and somehow ending up in these shabby neighborhoods, among people who meant me no good. Adults smile at such fears as unreasonable. But they are actually quite reasonable. No one is closer to the arbitrariness of one's station in life than a child; the hand is still so freshly dealt. A child has done very little that she can massage into personal mythology—into the idea that she has earned her position in the world.

As the train rolled into daylight, I reviewed the givens of my life: this family, this house, this hometown surrounded by farms, this school, and these friends. This nation of unquestioned superiority. This version of God. And this landscape: above all, this landscape. I felt basic, exceedingly normal. I was a child of small-town America, of the American Midwest. What were the odds, after all, of my identity being swapped? I pulled my coat tighter and waited to see more.

Usually we had breakfast at the Sheraton Hotel. Mom and Grandma, wrapping their hands around a second cup of coffee, wanted us to linger, to stay warm for as long as possible. It would be another hour, at least, before the stores opened. Charlie and I twisted on our stools, impatient to be off. Couldn't we at least go see the windows? There were Christmas displays, complex scenes with moving parts, and labels that took time to read.

Finally the women would relent. We found ourselves on Nicollet Avenue, our still-sleepy eyes fixed on singing elves and skating bears as we pretended not to mind the icy air. We kept close together; there were scarcely any people on the sidewalks yet, and in the street we saw only an occasional taxi. Even so, the pale winter light was getting stronger; life was coming on, and we four were the world's first inhabitants. We were getting the ball rolling in a frozen North American city.

We established a meeting post: If you got lost, come to such and such place at such and such hour. It was usually somewhere on the first floor of Dayton's department store, which seemed gargantuan and convoluted. In our quest for desirable things, we would now and then pass by the meeting place. It seemed to me that it was only ever found by sheer accident—that it would never disclose itself in the hour of actual need. A child a few hundred miles from home could therefore find herself in a serious pickle if she failed to keep track of her people.

I kept close to Mom or to Charlie if he and I were allowed an expedition to the toy department on our own. Sometimes, fascinated by a display, I would stop and let my lifeline to home wander out of view. These moments in which I was seemingly alone were tolerable, even intensely pleasurable, as long as they did not surpass a certain interval. It was as though I had an internal timer that would, at a given point, prompt me to seek a known face. Usually, I found Mom (or Charlie or Grandma) right away. But there were times when I would circle round and round, my alarm creeping upward as I covered every square foot of ladies' coats or children's shoes and spotted no one but strangers. Depending on the elapsed time between search and discovery, my body would flush with a mild or strong solution of anger mixed with relief.

The one time I did get seriously lost I do not recall in much detail. But I remember finding the meeting place and waiting there for what seemed like days. (I would not have been a small child at this point but an older one, permitted some range of movement as long as I stayed within the store.) I am sure I thought through every possible scenario: finding a friendly clerk to help (in one version, she takes me home to stay with her overnight); going to the police; simply being left in the store and locked in until morning (I find my way to the mattress department). Or I would be sent out by an apologetic but firm Dayton's security guard, expelled into the streets to meet an unimaginable fate. (Visions of the bad places: those desolate houses falling down, their hopeless inhabitants. Perhaps my excellent grades would slide; perhaps I would no longer even be sent to school but kept home and made to do wash.)

One day in the Christmas season not long ago, the memory of my worst-case imaginings returned. I saw a boy of about five barreling down the aisle of a discount store, sobbing as if his heart would break. I and every other adult in view knew immediately what was wrong (*lost!*) and dropped everything to see what we could do. Loping after the boy with deliberate calm, a half-dozen of us shortly saw him reunited with his mother near the checkout counter. She was young and open, enfolding her child (and, it seemed, his would-be protectors) in humor and reassurance. "See what happens when you wander off like that?" she told him—a lesson offered in easy tones, as if to say, Scary, yes, but nothing is ever so bad; I will always find you.

To my embarrassment, tears threatened my eyes; I tried to think why I was there. We protectors began to disperse but not before the boy could be seen heading for a card display. His mother, stuck in line, made her way nearer to the cashier. She shook her head. "He never learns," she said genially, to everyone and no one. She had her eye on him now but still emanated well-being, the way a small house lit with Christmas lights cheers a nighttime traveler.

In my own case, it was our friend Gordy Maxwell who had suddenly appeared, scattering my fears that I was in desperate trouble. We were sometimes joined in our Minneapolis excursions by friends of Mom's; this time it was Gordy and his mother. Hovering at the meeting place and shifting from one sore foot to the other, I saw Gordy: Gordy with a big "Ta-da!" grin on his face, the same as of a baby playing Peek-a-Boo. He was in the grown-up menswear coat his mother made him wear because this was the city. And he was glowing at me as though I were the final item on a scavenger hunt list.

Gordy could get on your nerves. He was a chubby kid who laughed too hard at things that were not that funny. But at that moment, he looked like an angel. Charlie was with him, but it is Gordy's big grin of recognition, with a glint of braces, that I remember. I told myself I would never think one bad thing about Gordy Maxwell ever again.

When I used to think of what heaven might be like, I supposed it was something like that experience of seeing Gordy. The first person you would see would not be your one true love but just some person you always knew, like Gordy Maxwell. "How's it going?" this person would say, and you would be amazed. "There's old Gordy Maxwell," you would think to yourself, "clear as day."

After that, it would be one glad recognition after another, as on the old TV show *This Is Your Life*. The band director. The minister. The clothing-store clerk who used to kid around with you. The girl in the next row at school whose lips moved when she read. The quiet boy who ended up in the state pen. You would just be so happy to see everybody, even people you thought you did not like, because they were your whole past. Your life. And you thought it was gone.

When I think of our country, I do not envision the entire United States. I think of a type of prairie farmland that straddles a few states and is shared by an us. In the early days of North American exploration, the Spaniards tried to make their move on our country by marching up from the south toward the nation's midsection. (These were the same Spaniards who brought the first horses and who, for that reason alone, were revered by me at an early age.)

More than once, the Indians led them deep into the plain, pretending they were showing the way to cities of gold. In fact, though, they planned to abandon the Spaniards on the unmarked land. One morning the Spaniards would wake to find the silence of the plain unnaturally amplified. It would take them a few minutes to grasp, in the clear, innocent light of morning, that they were ruined: not because of some threat bearing down on them— a painted war party or a cyclone—but because of an absence.

Their Indian guides had stolen away in the night, and they were doomed. Several Spanish parties disappeared in this fashion. Unable to find their way back to any recognizable point, they wandered in circles on the plain until they perished. The fear of becoming lost soon made the plain a thing to circumvent at all costs. It stayed that way for years.

Even today, someone will still occasionally get lost in a snowstorm. A high school boy on his way home from his job will leave his stalled car without wearing a warm hat or gloves and expire less than a mile from his house. Or someone with sharply reduced visibility will slide off the highway into a ditch. No one will come by until it is too late. The Midwestern prairie is no place to take for granted. But for me it felt and still feels like the safest possible place on earth. It is the only place where death, though certainly not welcome, might make a certain kind of sense. Anywhere else, death would be darkest abandonment, exactly the void our modern spirits are said to fear. But the vacancy of the prairie I trusted.

We only had the span of a day in Minneapolis. By the time we headed back to the depot, it was dark. Our feet ached, and we were no longer any match for the cold, which swept in from the unseen banks of the Mississippi River and gusted down the streets in icy plumes. The cold plunged deep into us and passed out again, as if we did not contain enough warm blood cells to occupy it. Our ears and noses and fingers burned, and though the women knew where we were headed, Charlie and I recognized no landmark and could see no end as we shifted our shopping bags from hand to hand. We would beg for a taxi and on some trips prevailed. Other times the women would say, "It's not far."

We sat for a long time in the station, our backsides growing sore against the polished wood benches, as we understood, finally, how bone-tired we were. The ceiling of the depot was so high. The light fixtures were ancient, as though from an old schoolroom. The heat had a singed ancient-radiator smell. Our eyes ached in the dry glare.

We waited for the train, our one and only, which left at about eight o'clock. The newsstand beckoned: one last chance to buy. Charlie and I, exhausted to the point of mania, left our bench to purchase gum—Juicy Fruit, Blackjack, or Beeman's flavored with clove. Then we twirled the tall racks displaying comic books. It lifted my spirits to know that home was out there—far away in the night yet somehow approachable, obtainable. The station itself symbolized this: The world was arranged so that people moving over vast distances could easily find their way. Moreover, and this was the most important part, we were with our mother: She knew how to get us to the one place that was right for us.

Though, like every child, I had peered into the opacity of my future, I had not yet heard of Tolstoy; I did not know how much my desires would one day run along the same track as his, or how, like him, I would never get over the God question. Nor did I know how small his prodigious talent would make me feel. Tolstoy would become a huge and immobile cloud billowing over my prairie. By the time he was forty-one, Tolstoy had unfurled his great epic *War and Peace,* peopling the world with the men and women of his imagination, not to mention five flesh-and-blood children of his own. By the time I was forty-one, I had bought a house and could not claim much else. I really could not account to myself for how I had spent all that time. But because I now lived near the train tracks, I would encounter the Tolstoy of Astapovo again and again in my imagination. These were disturbing reveries that always came to the same thing: I could not console myself that Tolstoy had come to a peaceful end.

In that prior time, though, in the icy night of Minneapolis, I was gloriously free of Tolstoy. I was a child of the American prairie waiting for the train home. My only longing was to complete the portage from station to train shed, and there to climb up into the passenger car, where we would at last stow all our closely guarded treasures. I could not wait to sink into the scratchy upholstery of seats dreamed up by the men of the Milwaukee Road.

Once on board, I gave in to exhaustion. I would wake occasionally in the dimly lit car and discern the figure of the Milwaukee Road warrior as the train charged across the prairie. Outside, it was practically burning with cold. Inside, we roasted and dozed. I found the warrior figure intensely romantic; his leaping-stag pose suggested movement and adventure. To me, he stood for freedom and power, for masculine beauty. He was utterly assured and assuring—a mysterious chief who would carry me home.

I remember only one arrival: a general rustling of people waking up; the conductor walking through to say our stop was next. My mouth was dry, and I was fuzzy with sleep. We collected our things. The train slowed and then halted with a small jerk. It was past midnight.

The conductor stood on the ground outside the train car to help us descend, first onto a short stool and then to the earth. He wore a blue wool suit and cap. He was powerful and important. He took my hand, said, "Watch your step" as my foot fished for the ground. I reached the stool, and then my foot, in its best Sunday-school shoe, plunged deep into a layer of new-fallen snow. I came to. The air danced with fluffy particles that were steadily massing into drifts. I looked down a deserted Main Street robed in white, its

Christmas decorations matted with snow and swaying in the wind. The cold was as pleasurable as a drink of ice water. I was alive with the sensation of cold and wrapped in the deepest enchantment we know, which is the strange familiarity of home.

SIXTH STREET

WHEN WE moved into our house in Eastboro, I knew nothing in the field of lawn-and-garden. I did not even know how to mow. But now, even though our house stood on less than a quarter acre, Andrew and I had a yard and trees we were responsible for.

We went down to City Hall for a presentation on composting. About a dozen people showed up, entrusting their attention to a man in a hat that said *Compost King*. He introduced himself, then immediately sat down in the front row. We all watched a videotape of him, the Compost King, explaining how to make compost out of lawn clippings, leaves, and kitchen scraps. You used the compost to enrich your soil, and it was much better for you and the earth than fertilizer.

Andrew and I were a little disappointed that the Compost King did not tell us everything in person, especially since he was right there. It would have been more natural, which is the whole idea behind compost. Still, we went home gung ho about composting and for at least a year faithfully carried our kitchen scraps out to the pile in the backyard. We had a chart taped to a cabinet door that told us which things could go. Eventually, though, we figured out that the compost would not just make itself. It had to be turned and watered. You had to dig it out from the bottom of the pile. Before long, without really saying much to each other, we had transferred our enthusiasm to the garbage disposal, a devouring In-Sink-Erator out of Racine, Wisconsin, which seemed far more eager than we could ever be to dispatch celery tailings and apple cores back into the wide world.

Now it is mostly yard debris that ends up in our imperfectly functioning compost pile. When the pile gets too high, we take some to the town compost center and add it to the communal pile. There, it is turned over by men with bulldozers, the true compost kings of Eastboro.

Knowledge did not come quickly. Fantasy did. I was going to have roses, delphiniums, peonies. I would fill the house with vases of cut flowers. Somehow, the stuff would just grow.

Yet for the first several months after moving in, I felt odd going into the yard. Years of apartment living had taught me that anything outside was out of bounds. Snipping a sprig of lilac where you rented was stealing. My territory was the interior. From the window of our new old house, I would watch our nearest neighbors briskly watering, trimming, planting, as if it were the most natural thing in the world. I felt funny even walking out into our yard to find out what we had.

One of the first things we put in was a climbing rose. I had stumbled across it in a fancy gardening catalog out of Connecticut. *Lillian Gibson Rose,* the catalog proclaimed. *Hardy . . . developed in North Dakota.*

My amazement at finding this personally significant rose, at the thought that I could buy it and have it bloom at my house in Massachusetts, was partly clouded by irritation.

"South," I apostrophized to the catalog. "South, south, south."

North Dakota, South Dakota—to some New Yorker living in Connecticut, what was the difference?

"So, how are things in North Dakota?" I have been asked often—by colleagues and coworkers and friends, by the parents of people I knew in college.

"South," I have said, smiling.

South, south, south. Never do I say what first comes to mind: "How the hell would I know? How the hell would I know what's going on in North Dakota?"

The Lillian Gibson rose is practically family. It was developed by a man I have always known simply as Grandpa Hansen. In Plainville, four of his great-grandchildren lived across the street from us and were playmates in the summer evening games called "Kick the Can," "Starlight, Moonlight," and "Run Around the House." In winter we attacked one another on the mountains of snow removed from the driveways, taking turns being king of the hill.

Grandpa Hansen was a distinguished professor of horticulture at South Dakota State University, in Brookings. He became known as the Burbank of the Plains for his work on plants that could survive the harsh weather where we lived.

The Lillian Gibson rose, named for the Gibson Girl of popular illustration, was the least of it. Grandpa Hansen came up with more than three hundred new kinds of plants designed to thrive on the American prairies and northern plains. He worked on everything from forage crops to fruits.

When Grandpa Hansen was a boy, the homesteaders in Dakota

Territory were desperate to find something that would grow there. It had to survive the Nordic winters and withering summers. This was no Eden, they had figured out right away. This was the place where everything came only with the greatest difficulty, where God repeatedly brought you to your knees and therefore almost always had your attention.

Niels Ebbesen Hansen came to the rescue. He was a Dane, and had arrived in the United States in the 1870s at the age of seven. It was a busy time in Dakota Territory: Dakota Southern brought the first railroad to the future state of South Dakota (the rails ran to Yankton, far south of us). Gold was discovered in the Black Hills, and the government engaged in a fierce war with the Sioux.

A plague of Rocky Mountain locusts came, followed by two years of grasshoppers just for laughs. Not knowing what else to do, the settlers fasted and prayed. Then they set fire to the prairie, so there would be nothing left for the grasshoppers to eat.

Even with all this going on, a boy could grow up and earn a degree at Iowa State College, in Ames, which is what Niels Hansen did. In 1895 he settled into his job as a professor of horticulture at SDSU.

That was the year, as nearly as we and the previous owners can determine, that workers started constructing our house in Massachusetts. Pictures from that time show new Victorians on cleared plots surrounded by nothing, as though at one time Eastboro contained pieces of prairie. In fact, our house vaguely suggests a farmhouse and, at the time of its construction, occupied the outskirts of town. There are no outskirts anymore in our section of southern Massachusetts, only town verging on town, and testy debates about development versus preserving "open space."

Once, when my parents came to visit, I picked them up at the Boston train station. We drove back to Eastboro in the dark.

"What are the crops around here?" Mom asked, peering out the window.

"Crops?" I said, feeling an eerie slide into displacement. "There are not really crops."

Somehow, the Northeast was like a thing you plugged in and it ran. There were a few apple orchards and dairy farms but mainly for cuteness. I lived in a place that had gone beyond crops. All that was left was lawn-and-garden.

Grandpa Hansen's great insight was that somewhere, nature had already supplied whatever it was that would grow in our drastic country. So beginning in 1897, he went out looking for it. He went to northern Europe, Asia, and Siberia. And there, after much searching, after bouts with cholera and pneumonia, not to mention encounters with robbers, he found it: the hybrid grain now known across the American plains as Cossack alfalfa. The plant he found shrugged off drought and all but welcomed blizzards. It was perfect for us. Grandpa Hansen collected a teaspoonful of seed and brought it home.

Soon the United States had a hardy new forage crop. All over the plains of western South Dakota, where, before, only short prairie grass would reliably grow, Cossack alfalfa was being planted for its seed. The seed was then sold and planted anew. For tillers of the soil, Cossack alfalfa was a triumph.

But for those trying to get their bearings, trying to understand the character of our home, the implications were hard to miss: *This place was like Siberia.*

Was that Grandpa Hansen's thought when he returned from

the steppes and gazed from the curtained window of his home in Brookings? Or did he have such hopes for Cossack alfalfa, for the upper Midwest as home, that the resemblance did not matter to him?

He was creating something immense, out of what must have been enormous faith in a vast, seemingly empty place. The Lillian Gibson rose he must have thrown in for kicks, after the more difficult work was done. The Lillian Gibson rose may be the faint breath of God's pleasure in the prairie. A tough little pink rose, with no fragrance to speak of, it endured—a sign, maybe, that God smiled on us, even as he hotfooted it out of there to cook up another calamity. Droughts and grasshoppers, tornadoes, blizzards and prairie fires the settlers had already seen. Dust storms were down the road. Grandpa Hansen would live to see these and to hear people ask: "What did we do wrong?"

There was no voice in the whirlwind then, only the wind itself, mere nothingness and loss.

Grandpa Hansen's descendants across the street, great-grand-children, were a boy and three girls. All were born in the 1950s. Mark, the oldest, was lean and intense, burdened with expectations. He was the quiet one in a house full of voluble girls. The girls, spaced two years apart in age, each had a different hair color, as if they were characters in a storybook. Meg, the oldest, had dark hair, nearly black; Maryann's was light brown; Martha's was flame-colored, an extraordinary red lit by strands of gold.

When she was very little, Maryann cut her bangs straight across at the root. It was the day of school pictures, and in the wallet-sized one we got, you could see the little tufts she left at the hairline, just above her forehead. She was the easygoing middle daughter, and her hair, in childhood, was short. But Meg and Martha had hair streaming down their backs, as if to emphasize more dramatic temperaments. Fingers flying, their mother would braid their hair in the morning, giving them each two long pigtails.

Their father, Doc See, was a veterinarian, Car One in his two-man partnership. He drove the country roads all day and could be radioed from the kitchen. The product of a farm near Brookings, he had a more-than-respectable tenor voice. On the basis of an audition tape, he had been accepted as a young man to Juilliard. Reluctantly, he decided that going there would be too impractical. So instead of heading to New York, he studied cattle and their diseases.

The mother, bearer of the Hansen genes, had been an official college beauty, as evidenced by the formals and yearbooks stored in a cedar closet in the attic. Even in summer, when it was so hot up there we could barely breathe, we children would go to the attic and look through things, performing our necessary archaeology among the mementos from Brookings. Periods of life passed away, we learned. But then you got a new one. In olden days, they wore corsages and stiff billowing skirts you could not even get your arms around. Meanwhile, make way for the new. Make way for us.

We tumbled downstairs, gasping for air, our faces red from the heat. The change of temperature thrilled us. We stood in front of the fan and lifted up our shirts. Outside, the sky was milky, the grass silver needles. It was August on the prairie, in the heart of the universe.

There were other Hansen hybrids, cousins who came from far away to visit in the summer. They had an air of having seen the world and looked us over with bored stares. For as long as they were visiting, we worshiped them. We were a cargo cult, with cousins as the cargo. One of the cousins went to MIT. I never heard the end of it. "My cousin who goes to MIT." What was MIT, anyway?

Somewhere out there was a world where children lived differently, where taxis and tall buildings were no surprise; where you could take ballet, compete in science fairs, go to MIT. City kids knew stuff you would never know. On the other hand, farms were strange to them. Farms were a novelty, a form of country amusement park. The visiting cousins worried that the animals would bite or trample them and were prissy about manure. How could you not look down just a little on kids like that?

The cousins believed they had come to a place of not-much-to-do. But they were wrong. They had come to Sixth Street, our street. When we said Sixth Street, we meant the neighborhood, which meant the world. Sixth Street contained every possible dream and therefore every possible experience. We were filled up, worn out by day's end. The prairie at our feet was the great stage of existence, and we felt free to use it as we pleased.

I knew all of the families and all of their houses, alternative universes that were somehow extensions of ours. The Miltons, across the street and down the block, had a round room in a small turret. "I've always wanted a round room," Mrs. Milton said with satisfaction, showing it off. The Camerons' kitchen smelled, depending on the time of year, of pickling or divinity. The Rasmussens' living room was the closest to something out of a magazine. It was immaculate, with thick wall-to-wall carpeting and Early American–style furniture. If you went to their house for dinner, they brought out beverages on a tray. The Rasmussens were like a TV family—Mom, Dad, and Jack; Jack, the godlike oldest boy in the neighborhood and automatic leader whenever he would deign to play with us.

Charlie and I played cards with the Nelson kids, Richard and Donna. "Who dealt this mess?" Donna would say. She was Daddy's girl; that was his line.

Richard, who like Jack had the authority of age, was a kind of junior impresario, arranging elaborate parades and costume dramas involving all the neighborhood kids. Other times he would sit at the piano playing "Alley Cat," declining to join in outdoor games that involved a lot of running.

Mr. Nelson had a way of scrunching up his face, so that his glasses took a ride on his nose, whenever he was staring at something far off. (Donna, in cat's-eye glasses, did this too. Her round nose was the same as her dad's, only with freckles scattered across. Her blond hair curled under.)

Mr. Nelson was doing this one warm summer day, was squinting out the front-door screen, when I was over playing with Donna. He scrunched up his nose as if something smelled. He was looking across the street at our house.

Donna and I were on the floor with a game. I remember a restless pacing that marred my concentration, and then Mr. Nelson was out the door, moving as fast as I had ever seen him go.

Donna went and looked out. "Your house is on fire," she informed me, the way one girl tells another her slip is showing. We ran out of the house and took up positions in her front yard.

Across the street, Mr. Nelson had found our garden hose and was spraying a smoldering heap in front of the garage. Balding and paunchy, he was in a vigorous action pose, working the hose, bounding around the smoldering pile like a cat. A fire truck, noisy and embarrassingly large, pulled up. I saw Mom coming around the side of the house from the backyard, where she had been drinking coffee with a friend. She was laughing. *Laughing!*

The fire department (who called?) was too late. Mr. Nelson had taken care of everything with the hose.

By this time, most of the neighborhood had come out to see. The cause of the fire was some old reels of film that had belonged to Grandpa Burges before he died. Mom had been cleaning the basement and decided to throw them out. The film, lying in the driveway, had caught fire in the hot sun while she was taking a break. Everyone was saying it was nothing; the fire had barely gotten started. But I stood there and cried. Our house. We could have lost it, lost everything we owned, and then what?

The former Laura Paulson, granddaughter of Niels Hansen, noticed me. Though I was a bit too old for it, she picked me up and carried me across Sixth Street to my mother, to my home. How could the visiting cousins know that everything worth mentioning in life happened here, including the threat of total conflagration? How could they know that Plainville was the world, with nothing beyond it at all?

Once, Charlie and I posed with the Nelson kids for our parents' movie camera. We stood lined up in front of their house, all holding Easter baskets. On the film, we just stood there smiling, dressed for church, holding our baskets. We were doing the self-conscious cute kid thing that the camera teaches you to do. Donna waved.

Of all the things our parents wanted to record, to memorialize that Sunday morning, we were it. Not budding trees or the houses lining the street, or, six blocks down, the prairie land spreading out like time; not the television sets or pianos or very latest appliances that greeted us when we went inside, and made it great to be an American; not robins, not dogs or kittens; not even cars, shiny and waxed and waiting in the driveway, ready to take us to

San Diego if we wanted, or Miami Beach. No; we were the whole show, the stars living there in Kid-Land, U.S.A.

The fact that we were on film meant that our stories were eternal. We were two brother-sister combos, and our stories would run alongside each other like train tracks. We were bound in the far-off future for Plainville High, a building we could see just two blocks away.

Then one day, the Nelsons packed up everything. Their station wagon sat by the curb, laden with their possessions. They were moving away. We would not see them anymore, or play with Richard and Donna again.

Mr. Nelson, it was said, had gone too far in disciplining a student at the high school, where he taught. It did not matter that some people took his side; he had to go. I was too young to understand the town politics that produced this day. But it was the first inkling I had that a very big thing other than a fire or tornado could go wrong, and you would not be able to do anything about it.

So the Nelsons' day of departure came, and we all stood on Sixth Street saying good-bye. We waved as they pulled out; their car moved down the street in the usual way, as if they were just going to get something at the store or maybe haul some stuff to the dump. When I could not see them anymore, I went inside and could not think of anything to play.

Once, we visited the Nelsons in their new place. They lived in Mankato, Minnesota, a bigger town with a new high school. We toured the school on an afternoon when it was empty, and were amazed. Mr. Nelson had a key and could go anywhere. He took us down long gleaming halls into classrooms full of new desks and the latest in lighting, also brand-new overhead projectors and a fully equipped chemistry lab. Everything was bright and clean. There was a lot of avid grown-up talk about facilities. Mankato had them.

The Nelsons still had their parakeet, the same one as in Plainville, who did not seem to notice he had moved. They kept him in the kitchen, in a cage on a stand. We kids played cards. "Who dealt this mess?" Donna said, wrinkling her nose in disgust.

We laughed a lot and were silly. We got competitive. Donna told on Richard, and the fun fell apart. I was eager to go home, even if it was not to superior facilities.

After that, I never saw the Nelson kids. Richard became a music teacher in Virginia. Donna stayed in Minnesota and worked for a radio station. Both married and had children. After leaving Sixth Street, the Nelson kids lived lives parallel with mine, witnessing all the same events of history—Kent State and Watergate, the oil crisis, and "Mr. Gorbachev, tear down this wall." They would have heard the same songs on the radio, gone through the same fashions in clothing and food. I have no images of them in disco days. I wonder if they log on to home computers or ever took up low-impact aerobics or cooking with tofu. I do not need to talk with them to know that in some way they are always looking for Sixth Street. Or maybe it is that Sixth Street looks for them.

A few years ago, Americans celebrated the fiftieth anniversary of the D Day invasion. There were documentaries and articles, a big reunion in Normandy of men who had lived through it.

"Guess who was on Omaha Beach?" Mom said during one of our Sunday phone calls.

I was sitting on the Jenny Lind bed Andrew had found in an antique shop in Indiana, before we ever met. He had stripped and restored it, polishing every knob and ridge, working the grime out of the indentations, so we could use it when we combined households.

"Who?" I said.

"Ray Nelson!"

I tried to picture Mr. Nelson: the way his glasses rode up when he squinted, his thinning hair brushed straight back, the snappy way he chewed gum. I pictured the man with the paunch, a dad, the only image of Ray Nelson I had.

Back then, Ray Nelson had been a Minnesota boy landing in France—France!—with the invasion's second wave. Everything I had read about lately I now saw through Ray Nelson's eyes: sunken equipment, the water running red, floating bodies; on the sand, more bodies, stray limbs.

Who dealt this mess?

Omaha was the worst, the one place not to be if you had to take part in this invasion. Aerial and naval bombardments that had been expected to help the troops there either fell far short of what was intended or did not occur at all. It was the same with the tanks, which either settled into the water or were blown up. Ramps of troop ships fell open, and the Germans machine-gunned whole squadrons before they could disembark. Some boats were swamped and the men simply drowned. On Omaha Beach alone, the Allies suffered an estimated two thousand casualties.

Those who made it onto the sand ran forward to a seawall and huddled there, realizing the choice was either to stay and be killed or ascend through unswept minefields and a barrage of enemy fire. Retreat was more dangerous still. Stunned officers sat on the beach, unable to take command. Someone later remembered that the bullets hitting the sand sounded like a person spitting out watermelon seeds back home.

To Allied officers watching from offshore that morning, Omaha looked hopeless. The reversal—dreamlike and uncanny to those who try to imagine it today, even to many who survived it—came when handfuls of men decided to try climbing the bluff rather than wait for death in the sand. It took most of the day.

There were a thousand versions of home on Omaha Beach that day, everyone wishing he were in that place instead. The cliffs of Normandy were as unlike home as anything could possibly be. No wonder Ray Nelson had a casual sense of safety after that, letting us ride on the back flap of the station wagon with our legs hanging out, watching, fascinated, as the road swept by under our feet. Mr. Nelson, creeping slowly on a gravel road out in the country, out to the dump, was the only father in the neighborhood who would let us do this. We loved it the way we loved a carnival ride, and we knew we would survive. So did Mr. Nelson. This, he knew, was nothing.

From time to time, we played army, falling down dead on our imperfect lawns, getting up again soon because the dry grass prickled and because it was boring to be dead. Half the time we did not even know which war we were playing: Civil War, cowboys and Indians, World War II guys. What was World War I?, I asked. The Germans again? Twice? We did not care, as long as there were two sides and we could divide up.

The summer after the D Day anniversary, Andrew and I visited the beaches at Normandy. Though it was late August, the day was cool and overcast. Even in a sweater, I shivered. We gazed down at the gun-metal sea from the high cliffs, where a viewing area for tourists has been constructed. It contains an explanatory placard with a map. Our eyes moved from the placard, up and down the coast, picking out the beaches: Utah, Omaha, Sword.

It was easy to picture the soldiers emerging from precisely this chilly gray mist, being dumped on the pitifully thin strip of sand far below. No home to go back to; no inn to beckon them forward; certainly no brochure describing the sights.

Yours, you know, looking down from the heights, is the advantage—an advantage so absurdly great that it is impossible to imagine the fool who would try this ascent. At our backs, the white crosses stood in row after row, a stupefying emblem of how the young invaders had, after all, achieved their goal, and a visual toting up of the price. They had scaled these inhospitable heights to a place where, years later, only green serenity awaited.

The soldiers' graveyard is mainly lawn, perhaps the lushest to be found anywhere on earth. Except in May or perhaps early June, no lawn in Plainville ever looked anything like it. Certainly no other lawn in France looked like this. Lawns are American. So is the invasion site on the cliffs of Normandy, given by the French to the United States in gratitude.

Andrew and I strolled through, unable to do anything about all this sacrifice, dazzled by grass that seemed to glow against the gray sky, an Emerald City of the dead. The magnitude of what had been done here by so many ordinary men—boys, really, who had never seen combat before—could not be understood. I focused numbly on the grass, thick and nearly flawless. After only a few years of home ownership, I could appreciate this achievement. Here was high skill, secrets of seed blends, fertilizer, and watering beyond my ken.

I spied a crew of groundskeepers, moving deliberately, unself-consciously about their work. "Well done," I thought, and aimed my camera their way. The groundskeepers dropped everything, then began mugging and waving. I started to laugh. *We are all alive! We can go home anytime!* We were big buddies in the dumb luck of peacetime. I snapped the groundskeepers' picture.

During one of the Midwest's periodic droughts, Plainville ordered water rationing. It meant you could water only every other day. The Hunter family had just built a new house on the edge of town, and a carpet of new sod, lush and green, had been installed at great expense. There were no shade trees yet; only the house, large and handsome, made of brick. And the lawn. Beyond that stood crops curling in the hot wind.

To keep their expensive new lawn alive, the Hunters were going to have to water every day. They braced for the fines and disapprobation, activating their sprinklers discreetly at night. By day the Hunters' lawn glowed in the baking sun. People drove by speechless with disapproval. They could not have been more astonished if they had stumbled across Versailles.

Great or small, the lawn is an emblem of a wish to be elsewhere. That is because, if it is not possible to be elsewhere, we refashion the existing terrain. It was just this impulse that drove Grandpa Hansen across the globe in search of hardy plants. He took a series of oxcarts through the steppes, submitting for weeks on end to the slow discipline of turn-of-the-century travel because he believed in upgrades.

The Hunters' lawn survived. Saplings went in and eventually offered a little shade. But for years the Hunters symbolized a kind of presumption their fellow townspeople had trouble dealing with. It was hubris to ask too much of the prairie and flat-out wrong to take more than your share. If God had intended a green world for us, he would have put us in the Cotswolds.

. . .

Before the prairie towns were laid out, before the countryside was ruled off into farms, the land was covered with tall grass. The tribes that passed through were hunting tribes. They did not envision any permanent structures, let alone any green lawns. Then the settlers came and broke up all the grasses with plows. Today, if you want to see native prairie grasses, you have to go to a special preserve.

Grandpa Hansen did not think about natural ecosystems or how to save them. His question was simply: How do we live here? And, after that: How do we get variety? There was so much land then and so much loneliness. The horizon was as awful as it was beautiful. A long life to you, it said; a long life, and then death. Our response, in a thousand ways small and great, was *You are telling me.*

No one who tried to make a go of it in the Dakotas needed Jean-Paul Sartre to point out that the foundation of being was nothingness. We could go out the door and see it for ourselves. No wonder the women knew ten craft projects for reusing Hi-lex bleach jugs, along with any number of other ways to keep busy. We lived smack dab on the rim of nothingness, and it was neither polite to bring it up nor safe to dwell on the fact. In sod-house days, we knew, the sameness had frayed some people's minds. Hardship and loneliness finished them off.

I once read that to go insane is to lose variety: a person can think only of the one thing—one thing exclusively, all day long. If so, Grandpa Hansen's career could be seen as a long fight to save his sanity and ours. In all, between 1894 and 1934, he made eight trips to Europe and Asia. During one of them, he arrived in Russia to find the old order collapsing. The czar and his family had been moved out of their palace, and people of all kinds were going inside, roaming about at will. Such a temple to variety they had not seen.

According to family lore, Grandpa Hansen went in too and was astonished to see people helping themselves to whatever they found. It was useless, at such a time, to speak of what was right; Grandpa Hansen had come looking for hardy alfalfa and instead found himself at one of the greatest loot-fests in history. He took a small teacup and shipped it home. Today the czar's cup occupies a cherished shelf in a farmhouse at the end of a gravel road in South Dakota. If they think of it, the descendants of Grandpa Hansen bring it out to show visitors and tell its history, handing on the tale with care.

Because of Grandpa Hansen, thousands of acres of alfalfa were planted in our unpromising country. And, of no less importance to me, I had someone to play Barbies with.

Meg and I had the original ponytail Barbie, with vamp's eyes. We had bouffant Barbie, bendable Barbie, Ken, Midge, and Skipper. I had Ricky and Scooter, Skipper's friends. We had official carrying cases for the dolls and their clothes. We had Barbie beds with pink canopies.

Our favorite thing was to amass our Barbies and their paraphernalia in Meg's living room or ours, then to play intensively for two days or more, as if we were on Barbie retreat. We had to get special permission to lay everything out. Several hours later, by some mysterious accord, we would strike the set.

We created a floor plan. Cases propped open served as room dividers; so did shoes and blocks. We covered the entire floor with Barbie village. The same impulse to create a world, and make it complete, expressed itself in the fall when, on someone's lawn, the children of Sixth Street would use raked-up leaves to outline a house. We marked off the rooms with long straight borders. We came and went, entering only through the breaks that signified doorways, as on an architectural floor plan.

One day, just like our parents, we would have houses. We would understand about furnaces and washing-machine hookups. It seemed both impossible and as inevitable as entering the next grade. How could it be otherwise? We came from families in houses.

We did know a few single people, mostly women who taught. Miss Myrtle, Miss Larkin, Miss Wallace. We supposed we would not end up like that—in tidy apartments with a few well-placed doilies. Apartments, though there were a few in town, were not the usual way to live. They were a subworld, make-believe, with kitchens that looked like play kitchens. Apartments were kid worlds with no kids.

Nevertheless, when we played house, I could not exactly picture myself as the mother. The baby dolls I owned, with giant plastic heads, were more like fixtures—curtains, maybe—than spirits, whereas all my toy horses truly lived, stomping and shifting in the closet, impatient to get out of their shoe boxes on Saturday morning. And though I had a Barbie, I was somehow never her. I was maybe Midge, the friend, a freckled tomboy, incongruously stacked (conveniently, she had the same body as Barbie, which meant they could swap clothes). Midge looked in on all the drama of Barbie's life with a bright plastic smile. She was helpful, well adjusted, and thoroughly beside the point.

It was Barbie, not Midge, who had the dream house.

In fifth grade, we studied the fifty states: state bird and state flower, capital city, principal products. Our teacher said we might live in one of the other states one day. In idle hours we fantasized and chose. Little Rhody, we all effortlessly remembered, was the smallest state, a little joke of geography. Beyond that, what was there to it? A rooster. Big doings during colonial times.

Texas, on the other hand, I could see. That was where the cowboys were. In Texas you had not farms, like we had, but ranches. In Texas you could not do without horses. Texas was probably where Roy Rogers and Dale Evans were. I was all in favor of Texas.

It was Meg who ended up there, following a local boy to San Antonio during the big Sunbelt boom. Texas needed teachers, and we sent them a bunch, even while thinking Texas did not especially deserve South Dakota's principal product, which was its serenely balanced young people, packing common sense in one holster and a solid work ethic in the other.

The local boy got a good job at a huge new high school. But in the end, he did not comprehend the life story Meg was composing for herself. Meg wound up married to someone else, a doctor so thoroughly native that she had no trouble thinking of him as Mr. Texas. He knew as much about the Alamo as you were willing to hear, and more after that.

They were comfortable, in a sprawling one-story house with a pool out back that gleamed like a slab of turquoise. When I visited, Meg and I went to the Alamo and then to the River Walk, where in a mood I could not ever explain, we bought matching cowgirl outfits, hers in olive and mine in blue, our choices coordinating with the color of our eyes. The outfits came from a boutique where dress-up Western wear blended with the latest fashions in a form of chic confined largely to Texas. I wore mine around Rhode Island anyway; I wore it to my job on the night copy desk, where it was no more strange than a lot of other people's attire. (One woman wore black leather from head to toe, while another favored a purple jogging suit.)

After touring the Alamo, Meg and I had a nice lunch with wine. We had a great time. It was spring, Fiesta week, and already people were wearing the official T-shirt, which showed a kind of neon Keith Haring–style Alamo.

I loved San Antonio: the rococo blend of cultures; the flat landscape that held it all together; the fragrance of the fajitas in the old marketplace, where I was promised the best margarita of my life, and it was so.

Meg was something like society in her new home, and yet she had somehow reproduced the atmosphere of middle-class thrift and discipline I remembered from Sixth Street. She sewed Christmas and Easter dresses for four daughters. She refused to spend X dollars on designer jeans or sneakers, even though they could afford it, because, as she explained to me, that kind of extravagance was just wrong.

The three older girls, products of Dan's first marriage, were trained to help clear the table and clean up, just as Meg and her sisters had done. They hovered in the kitchen while we talked, thinking, as girls do, they might pick up something useful to know.

Ann, the oldest, absently repeated a set of cheerleader motions, in a kinetic memory that reminded me of Meg at that age; *B, B, B-u-l-l, D, D, D-o-g-s, bulldogs bulldogs BULLDOGS.*

Meg told me about her dream: She and I were flying above Sixth Street, but we could not get into the houses. We could not find anybody. We flew up and down, looking. Only our two houses were in color; all the others were ash-hued with stone markers outside. Tombstones?

It was a sad dream and a recurring one. She always woke from it feeling disconsolate.

Without question, she was grateful for her new life; money

was not a problem, as it had been in the land where most of our parents played the same game of trying to press water from a stone. But here, the girls could not walk to anything; they had to be driven. And the material outpouring at Christmas was, to Meg, not only unseemly; it produced less happiness rather than more.

Neither of us knew whether the comparative richness of our own childhood was real or imagined—the Edenic projection that is part of growing older, of growing more estranged, even as the world becomes less surprising, more tediously familiar. But I understood her dream. Meg was a doctor's wife, active in church and the Junior League, a pillar of her new community. Yet like me, she was in exile, a resident alien in her own country.

Not long ago *The Wall Street Journal* carried an article about water use in San Antonio. A local newspaper had begun listing the city's top ten water hogs—people who were using tens of thousands of gallons per month to keep their lawns green during the summer. Theirs is the same dream of a different country we had in South Dakota. The dream brought us Cossack alfalfa and the Lillian Gibson rose: the rose acknowledging that yes, our home was not an English country garden, but that said, all the same, Stay. *There is a variety of beauty that is sturdy and kind and takes no more than it needs. It is enough.*

Around 1913 the South Dakota legislature appropriated ten thousand dollars for Grandpa Hansen to buy seed in Russia and Siberia. By 1919, 462,000 acres of the northern plains had been planted with strains he brought back. In a report that year he wrote:

"My conclusion from all this alfalfa work is that if each western state could get a million acres of our driest uplands into the right kind of alfalfas and certain other drought-resistant plants, it would prevent the usual exodus of disappointed settlers."

In short, don't give up on this place. That was his work and the meaning of his life. And thanks to his help, they pretty much got it nailed down: a state of about seven hundred thousand people, with an economy heavily based on agriculture. And still we dispersed, like seeds, from Sixth Street, in a process that seemed to undo Grandpa Hansen's great project.

REGINE

WHEN JOE DiMaggio died, one of the headlines read: YANKEE
CLIPPER SAILS FOR HOME. The headline writer should have gotten
a bonus that week for making a tired metaphor do double duty.
Home plate and our final resting place rolled into one. Not bad
for one of those eye-burning, soul-shrinking crank-it-out nights
on the copy desk.

Heading home is death's ultimate cliché. Yet even if we know
this, it sticks, like gum on the bottom of a shoe. Why is it so hard to
shake the idea that dying equals going home—that we are bound
for a home beyond home? The notion that we have forgotten our
true home, which is in eternity, goes as far back as the Greeks in the
time before Christ. Later on, it animates the neo-Platonists and
freights the poetry of Wordsworth. It is the elusive bird singing in
Heidegger's deep woods. The Christian imagery of my childhood is
full of the going-home idea. In Bible school we sang a song: "We're
going to a mansion on the Happy Day Express. The letters on the
engine spell J-E-S-U-S." The point of the song is that you are supposed to want to go there; you cannot wait to board the train.

Maybe it is simple. Because home is the most comforting of all ideas, we place it imaginatively at the end of life. In so doing, we neatly spare ourselves the stark terror that comes with the thought of mere disintegration. Whether we created religion or religion created us does not matter. We simply need a bearable picture of the end. And so we think of home.

At my Grandpa Andersen's funeral, the pastor attributed these words to him: "The ship is nearing the harbor, and Jesus, the pilot, is on board." The pastor seemed deeply affected by this statement, allegedly uttered to him in private during Grandpa's final days. All around me I heard sobs.

I was thirteen and had never heard Grandpa Andersen say much one way or the other about Jesus. Certainly he had little to say about ships. It was Grandma who was the religious one. She could not get enough of church and spent hours there, often dragging my poor dad along when he was little, because he was the youngest. From what I could tell, Grandma prayed almost constantly. She asked the most convincing table blessings I ever heard, each time making me feel truly grateful for the food. It was because of her that I understood the implicit sacrifice of animals, which, like Jesus, gave their lives so that we might live. Because of her, I cannot even unwrap a piece of chicken from the market without feeling both an upsurge of reverence and a sense of my unworthiness.

On hearing Grandpa's valedictory words, I felt a little disappointed in him. He had stood in my mind as the largely secular hero of farm life, a person for whom many questions remained open. (Never mind that for me, at that age, the big ones were settled.) Had he been so badgered by pastoral visits at the end that he finally gave in? Had trite metaphor been urged on him until it seemed like his own idea? Or were the words real, signifying a true conversion for which he lacked more interesting language?

The ship is nearing the harbor.

Had Grandpa Andersen ever even seen a harbor? Unlike his Danish immigrant parents, he was born on the prairie, so far from any harbor that the sea must have seemed a mythical construct to him. The sea was a dragon, whereas what Grandpa Andersen knew were hogs. I believe the farthest away from South Dakota Grandpa Andersen ever got was Denver, Colorado. He visited by car with Grandma on their honeymoon. Her parents came along, since a car was going out that way. That must have been fun.

My view, even in childhood, was that Grandpa was not cut out for God. He farmed and played the fiddle. "Oh ya, Pete could play anything," Uncle Russell told me long after Grandpa was gone. This was news. I had never seen Grandpa play; I had never even seen a fiddle in the house. And like any child visiting, bored, I had probed every corner, had hidden in the closets and buried my face in the talcum-powder smell and feel of Grandma's dresses.

When he knew he was dying, Grandpa said to Grandma: "Now you'll be able to marry that preacher you always wanted."

You could hear the hurt in her voice when she told it; could hear that she never wanted anyone but him. Only why hadn't he wanted God the way she did? If only they could have straightened that part out, for of course she was right. It was one stubborn Dane against another. To keep herself sharp, Grandma would lie in wait for the Jehovah's Witnesses, peeking from the curtain as they came up the walk, her Bible at the ready. When they came inside, she pounced, arguing lengthily, matching them verse for verse. The Jehovah's Witnesses could not get out of Marie Andersen's house fast enough.

Once, when we visited her in the nursing home, Grandpa was

all she could think of. "Where's Pete?" she said. He had gone off with some other woman, she suspected; that was why he was not here.

Grandma and Grandpa Andersen lived in the same rural township all their lives. It was predominantly Scandinavian, almost exclusively populated by farmers. The town at its center, barely a town, was a dip in the road the founders had named Regine, and which sat on the convergence of three counties. I loved the approach to Regine: first, field after field; then the sudden descent, an inverted bell curve. Surprise! A town! Entering Regine brought a stomach-dropping, roller-coaster thrill. From our earliest days, Charlie and I were connoisseurs of variations in the terrain, and the entrance to Regine was one of the most notable we knew. From this alteration in the land had come our father, and hence us.

Just as Minneapolis was the City, Regine was the Other Town, alternative townness. By offering contrast, Regine exposed the advantages of the town where we lived. In my earliest years, it proposed the strange idea that Plainville was not the center of the world. The people of Regine, South Dakota, went about their lives in much the way people in Plainville did, though on a smaller scale. They seemed untroubled by the fact that their Main Street lacked clothing and hardware stores, or by the narrow range of choices in the two places that sold groceries.

In Regine were children who did not know about me or the kids in my class and who mistakenly worshiped their town's homecoming queen, not knowing that the real and true queen, the only one worth envying, was in our town. Regine children had funny words for things. What we called barbecues (ground beef in sauce on a bun), they called taverns. When my cousins said, "Want to go down to the station?" they meant the gas station. Regine had no train station.

Nevertheless, Dad was a kind of star there. Everybody knew him when he came home and said, "Hello, Lawrence," a name he was not called in Plainville. He had been the valedictorian of his high school class—and so what if that class numbered only twenty-eight. Number one in Regine was a big deal, in Regine.

Regine was an argument for the fragility of towns. It seemed to have only one of everything: one school, one general store, one bar, one gas station, one newspaper office, one post office. Beyond the town lay nothing. In fact, nothingness bore down upon Regine, threatening to engulf it, especially in summer. Blue skies, flat blond or green fields, silence. The stark dress of winter and the unfocused expectations of Christmastime made the countryside more tolerable. But even in that enlivened season, the industrious motion of Plainville was missing, at least from what I could tell.

Because of Regine, I understood the problem of the tavern. I knew that the drinking of the men was connected to the billowing beyond, to the epic vacancy of our shared country. The God-sense of the women flowed from the same source. There had to be something, their hearts insisted; otherwise the whole setup was just plain mean. These leanings—toward drink or toward God—represented the extremes. They beckoned on the outskirts of the town and were appreciated by all. Mostly, the people of Regine lashed themselves to the mast and kept on an even keel. Ordinarily, neither church nor tavern claimed too great a share of their souls. Their energy was channeled by farm life, by the demands of crops and livestock. It was good, at noon, to sit down and have dinner (dinner was the midday meal, supper the evening). It was good to take a ride into town; to buy some stamps and some groceries; to have a bottle of pop and see who all was there. The kids whizzed through school, competing in basketball and band, then going off to college at Yankton or Vermillion, and sometimes even farther away, to Iowa or Nebraska. When they came back for reunions, it was often to a gathering of several classes at once, or even of the whole town. Otherwise why bother?

I felt profoundly safe in Regine. It was where my family went to watch the confused footage of the Kennedy assassination; the subsequent funeral pageant; the killing of Lee Harvey Oswald, which prompted Dad to rise from Grandpa's easy chair, exclaiming, "They shot him!" just when my toy horses—the blacks, the bays, the fiery whites—found good grazing near Grandma's out-of-tune piano, causing me to miss television history.

As I would notice over and over, something in the world beyond the prairie made people act up, whereas any crazed killer who made it to Regine would surely run out of motivation. I knew this because of the way Regine drained energy from Charlie and me the minute we arrived. We sat with the uncles and aunts in the tiny living room, ate another cookie or small sandwich as another plate of food was passed. The uncles were slow and amiable, with skin ruddy from the sun. The aunts, all in dresses with self-belts, made a brisk business of doing the dishes every few hours.

Charlie and I slipped into a daze as the adults brought up people we did not know. There were pauses into which you could have fit entire towns. I marveled at Dad's ability to find topics. "Why don't you go outside?" Mom would say, noting our stupor. But we could think of nothing to do there. As a formula for subduing children, Regine might have bottled itself.

In the tiny upstairs bedrooms, with their slanted ceilings, aged wallpaper, and framed verses devoted to Mother, we slept deeply, heavily, as though in some spa interlude meant to ground the soul in Americana. Charlie and I were usually assigned to the park room. It contained a hand-tinted portrait of Dad as a young man and a double bed made of tubular steel. The bed was painted mud-gold. It was, for a child, a running-start bed, so high Charlie and I needed some momentum to leap onto it. From the bed we could look out the window and see the town park. It had been built for baseball and was partially surrounded by a stone wall wide enough to walk on. We walked the wall every time we visited. It was the one activity we knew of in Regine. At the far end of the park, where the wall ended, was a pasture. Sometimes cows stepped up to the fence and stared. We stared back.

The cows seemed full of Regine—as if nothing had occurred to them in life and never would. We knew there were other places, though—Plainville; the great city of Minneapolis. The weatherman on TV would tell of still more places: Sioux Falls and Sioux City and Valentine, Nebraska. Bismarck, North Dakota. I understood that we did not have to lock gazes with the cows forever. And yet there always seemed a moment in this fixed exchange that implied no escape. The world was reduced, and plain.

I remember waking one morning in the park room when I was no longer a child. I had been out into the larger world and come back with my expanding satchel of fears. A soft breeze lifted the voile curtains, and birds were singing. Beyond the park, I knew, were the sounds of the farm, of many farms: cattle with their velvet step thudding across the earth; chickens, their clucking like the sound of eggs jostling in boiling water; the rasp of trees in motion; breakfast sounds; the radio. It was a version of peace, my version, I understood then. I focused intently, trying to gather it in.

It was this peace that I wanted for my own house someday. And some years later, anticipating this essential but impossible fulfillment, I insisted that the bed from the park room be saved. Grandma was moving to the nursing home and was selling as many of her things as she could. "Not the bed," I said, calling home, sounding the family-heirloom warning bell.

I could not get home for the sale, but Dad honored my wish without quite understanding it. "The mattress is shot," he pronounced. He wanted to throw it out. I reluctantly said okay. Dad found men at the lumberyard in Plainville who were willing to build a crate for the frame. They were so proud of the crate when they were done that they signed it.

The crate with the bed inside was put on a truck, a "common carrier" bound east with assorted things heading to assorted households. I do not know how many destinations it hit, how many determined notions of material necessity it fulfilled, before stopping, finally, outside my apartment building in Providence. I had the bed painted gray and ordered a custom-made mattress for it.

"What would she want with that old bed?" Grandma Andersen asked. It was only after I had made my bid, insisted that the bed be saved, that I found out Dad had been born in it; that his brother Dale, while very sick, had undergone a religious conversion experience in it; that another family member had died in it. This was a bed with authority.

In our house in Eastboro, the bed occupies the guest bedroom. I like seeing it, like dressing it up with old quilts and vintage pillowcases. While I was living alone, sleeping in it every night in three successive apartments, the bed gave me a greater sense of well-being. But it has never re-created the sense of deep calm, of absolute security, I felt waking up in it in Regine.

Memory is no substitute for the place we have journeyed from—the actual place, with its people, sounds, and scents, its precise angles of light, its exact breezes. I can sit in my house in Eastboro and picture the little white frame house in Regine, the prairie land extending beyond, and be quite glad about it. But I can never reach the state I was in on that morning, when I belonged so completely and with such complete trust to the reality of Regine.

For all I know, Grandpa was tired of Regine by the time he entered the ominously named Sunset Manor. It was in the nursing home that he began to speak of harbors. But I believe that whatever force overcame him there is the same as the one that led Tolstoy to create Levin, and Levin, in his turn, to create Tolstoy.

For my grandmother, Grandpa's ending was surely a victory. The surprise was how unconsoling it turned out to be, and what a forsaken landscape it made of her prairie.

DUTCH COLONIAL

OUR HOUSE in South Dakota was a Dutch colonial, from the outside okay-looking but never in my eyes beautiful. It was light gray, then maroon red, malted-milk brown, and finally, after I left, a deeper shade of brown that made me think of Swiss chalets. The trim was white. It was Mom's childhood house, specially built for her family. She moved in as a little girl, left for college, married, and moved back when I was a little girl.

Thanks to my Aunt Mildred, the family's indispensable historian, I own a photocopied picture of another Dutch colonial, completed in Clara City, Minnesota, in 1912. This one was built by Cornelius Burges for what would become a family of nine children, mostly boys. The one who stands alone in the foreground of the picture, in knickers and a cap, is Charles, the second oldest and my mother's father.

Like so many constructions of its era, the Clara City house appears isolated, standing alone on a bare plot of land. Except for my grandfather, the family members (only six at this point) are arranged on the porch, which features simple white columns. Other charming details abound: leaded glass windows, scalloped shingling, an oval window just under the eaves, like the jewel in an Indian woman's forehead. A potted palm has been brought onto the porch for the photograph and constitutes the only real planting at this point. A white dog, vaguely bearlike, sits in an alert pose at the foot of the front steps.

Cornelius Burges had come to this area of southern Minnesota by covered wagon while still a boy. The Burgeses were among a number of Dutch families attracted to Chippewa County; what would they build but Dutch colonials? Charles Burges, thus launched, must have felt that nothing said home quite like a Dutch colonial, and so, like his father, he had one made, though with less ornamentation, in Plainville. And thus we came to live under a Dutch colonial's trademark hipped roof, so evocative of the nation's barns.

The thing my mother most wanted in life was to stay home in this house. I knew her fantasies by the magazines that arrived. They showed women waxing their floors with new Glo-Coat and whipping up meals with the help of electric frying pans. The women of today planned backyard luaus in summer and dived into Christmas crafts projects when it turned cold. For instance, using felt, you could make your daughter a skirt exactly like a Christmas tree skirt. You could make a decoration for your doorknob that jingled when someone came inside.

But Mom had her job at the newspaper, along with a shifting assortment of civic duties: study club member, church organist, worthy matron of the Order of the Eastern Star, guardian to Job's Daughters. All over town, women got to stay home and be housewives. Even more compelling, so did June Cleaver on TV and Doris Day in the movies. Imagine a full day of ordering groceries, dusting until everything gleamed, and then, at the conclusion of dinner, presenting a lovely chilled dessert in a stemmed glass.

Mom was bursting with domestic fantasies: a new color scheme for the small back bedroom; a clean garage; all the clutter boxed, labeled, and shelved, turning our family into a kind of museum of itself.

Instead, Mom had to work.

Our stuff was everywhere. Dirty dishes sat out. Laundry mounded on the closet floors. You could inscribe SOS in the dust on our end tables. Mom could never, she felt, keep up.

Mom had been a high school valedictorian who eloped midway through her college career at the University of South Dakota. She would have kept going, but it was an era of imprecise birth control. By the age of twenty-one she had two babies. First came Charlie, then me.

"You'll never finish college now," her mother announced, in a prophecy meant to shake the family tree.

Lucille Burges, née Whittom, knew her daughter. She knew the lurking sense of inadequacy that yoked her relations one to another, going all the way back to (she claimed) Daniel Boone. To counter this, our hearts beat with a certain "I'll show you" arrhythmia. It was passed down like eye color. *I'll show you.* My mother transferred her studies to South Dakota State, closer to the town where we lived and where my father had his first job teaching music.

Amid diapers and bottles, Mom did course work, supplementing Dad's meager earnings by giving piano lessons. When she completed her degree, as Lucille Whittom had known she would, Charlie and I were both there. Dressed in our best Sunday clothes, we were photographed inspecting a cannon on the campus where our mother, still in her early twenties, was graduating Phi Beta Kappa.

. . .

It is Betty Friedan who most often gets the credit for identifying home as women's prison. This would have bewildered my mother, if she had ever bothered to read Betty Friedan. When I was growing up, the "women's libbers" were a distant disturbance, something joked about in our town. The bra burnings that got most of the attention offended my sense of modesty, so I inquired no further. As an adolescent, I was afraid to wear white blouses, which could hint at the outline of the implicating garment underneath. The thought of one of the boys reaching to snap the back strap was enough to sear me with humiliation. There should be no visible sign that such a thing even existed. Still less should it be a prop at a rally.

Betty Friedan would have said that what looked like the bad hand dealt to my mother—her economic need to work—was actually a good one. Work gave her independence, competence, and dignity, some status in the world.

Mom would not have had time to hear this. Her work load seemed to expand each year. The long hours became longer. The multiple tasks multiplied. Mom took most of the pictures for the paper and covered the city council meetings, long sessions that wound late into the night. The men of the council, and the gasbags who had business before them, leisurely uncoiled their thoughts, loving their own words, making monstrous sport of my mother's industriousness. Arriving home past midnight, she would be up after only a few hours' sleep to write the story, ensuring that the city council proceedings made it into that week's issue.

Although she rarely had time to think about it, Mom had a tradition to uphold. After stints in seminary, business college, and school teaching, Cornelius Burges had gone into the newspaper business. In 1895 he bought the *Chippewa County Herald*, re-named it the *Clara City Herald*, and ran it for thirty-eight years before retiring to St. Paul. Three of his sons—Ted, Charles, and Harold—entered the newspaper business. Charles bought our paper, the *Herald Advance*, in 1931. When he died of a stroke in 1957, Grandma became the publisher. My parents moved to town temporarily to help, and the temporary part fell away. Before they knew it, they were running the business.

Outlandishly, there was a competing weekly in our town, *The Prairie Sun*, with a history almost as long as the *Herald Advance*'s, and also with a woman editor. Like Mom, Victoria was running a paper inherited from her father. Like Mom, she was determined to keep the thing going. Once, Dad walked down Main Street and into the *Sun* office and pointed out that this was nuts. The papers should combine.

The answer was: Nothing doing. Who would be boss?

And so our town of thirty-five hundred people, sitting isolated on the prairie, had two weekly newspapers. From one point of view, this was an improvement: In the 1880s, before the town barely had a chance to think of itself as a town, there had been four.

After I moved to the Northeast, people in the newspaper business would whistle with amazement when I told them what was going on in my hometown. In major markets all across the country, competing big-city dailies were folding, leaving only one newspaper to care for the doings of hundreds of thousands of people. The loss of competition was widely lamented. It would have been news to Mom and Victoria, and about as relevant to them as whatever Betty Friedan was saying. They were locked in the most vicious of all struggles, which is the struggle for low stakes. And neither one could see any end to it.

"They've got to eat too," Dad would say from time to time.

Once, I heard that Victoria had said the same thing: "They've got to eat too."

"*They*?" I said, incredulous. "*They're* 'they.'"

Mom cooked and sewed and cleaned. She was good at all of it. Sewing was how she showed she cared about me. Once, in grade school, we were instructed to bring something from home for a display on colonial times. I wanted to make my Ken doll into Ben Franklin but did not know how. I was frustrated, gave up, and went to bed.

In the morning, there was Ken, in knee breeches and a white shirt with lace at the throat. He wore an orange printer's apron. His black plastic Wingtips had been transformed by tiny silver grommets into buckled shoes; he had tall white knee socks. Some other doll's cowboy hat had been raided, glued to make it three-cornered, and hair from a blond wig had been snipped and fastened to the back, tied at the end to give young Ben Franklin a ponytail.

Mom had stayed up till three finishing it. Ben Franklin was the hands-down hit of the display case, which was in the hall for the whole school to see.

She fried chicken. She made cheese fondue. She rolled her own crusts for peach pie. She made a gingerbread house once and glued it together with white icing. She baked bread, caramel rolls, and Bundt cakes. When she was done, the kitchen sparkled; the house smelled good. Mom would sit on the davenport and leaf through a magazine, and anyone could tell she felt happy.

Sometimes I helped decorate for Christmas, but what I liked most was to come home and find what Mom had done. The main part of the house, Grandma's part, was the best canvas, and Mom used it, arranging clusters of pillar candles and greens, filling glass bowls with ornaments that matched the soft blue color scheme, positioning the crèche in semi-darkness, so that its literalism faded and its symbolic beauty filtered through the house. Even kitschy items she was able to position artfully so that they charmed, intimating a past beyond my own, introducing me to nostalgia.

I would walk in on Mom's version of Home for the Holidays, everything freshly dusted, polished, and vacuumed, and feel a blast of happiness. Our house was so beautiful. I loved our house.

Mom tried to figure out ways to steal time for her domestic life. For work, she decided, the answer was a wig. She did not have the time or money to keep getting her hair done, especially the time. She had to get up in the morning and go. She had to be in the office early, making calls and writing up the news. (She could type, fast, on her big humming electric, with the phone cradled on one shoulder.)

We went to Minneapolis, and Mom was in the wig department at Dayton's for a long time trying on. She picked out a wig that was soft brown with a hint of red. It was cut feathery and full. It had its own black patent leather case and a white stand shaped like a head.

Mom was careful with it when we got it home. We were all careful around the wig. Sometimes, when she wore it, Mom looked to me like someone familiar but in a play.

Unlike most of the mothers I had seen visiting our class at school, Mom had a small, trim figure. She wore short dresses and tall fashion boots with heels. She figured the boots could double as snow boots, saving time. The boots reminded me of Nancy Sinatra, who had a hit song about then, "These Boots Are Made for Walkin'."

By the time I reached high school, Mom and I could have worn a lot of each other's clothes. We had the same shoe size. She bought a pair of shoes in a color called new red that went with a lot of her things but more of mine. New red was tomato red, and it was all over Minneapolis that year. Eventually, I had the new red shoes. Mom didn't mind.

She sewed a lot of things I thought I really wanted—let me pick out the fabric and hemmed the skirt as high as I liked. I would wear things for a while, and when they failed to change who I was—failed to give me a new life at the high school—I would let them sit in the closet: good clothes that Mom had spent hours making, including a madras plaid jacket I needed because everyone had one.

Mom did not say too much about this casual abandonment of her efforts, this abuse of her time. I was as bad as any crank who appeared before the City Council and went on and on.

I would propose the next garment.

"Will you wear it?" she would ask. She would scrutinize my face, give me a hard, skeptical look.

I insisted I would wear it. That was about the extent of her resistance.

Mom's early efforts to teach me to sew, when I was ten, did not go well. I cried with frustration, did not care about sewing. The fabric puckered when I tried to cut it. Mom said I was old enough to learn, to make my own sleeveless summer dress for the trip we were planning out west to visit Dad's two brothers.

It was war—against the facings at the armholes, the ruffle at the bottom, the zipper. When it was done, I hated that dress—a print in pale blue and pink and brown, with a white background, fresh-looking and sweet. It reminded me of Mom's will and the unhappy hours of its making. The work was sloppy, not as good as Mom's. I wore the dress in California because Mom insisted.

After that, Mom gave up on teaching me to sew. I learned later, in home ec, on the high school's clunky plastic Singers. I started to like it. In the summer, to keep ourselves occupied, my friend Andrea and I would sew up a storm. We made caftans and summer dresses, pant-skirts and shorts with matching tops. We picked out fabrics for fall to keep time from stopping—the time that unfurled like endless miles on the prairie; time that made you feel you were not getting anywhere at all.

The summer after we finished fifth and sixth grade, Charlie and I went to church camp in the Black Hills. With a few other kids from our congregation, we left very early in the morning, on a school bus, stopping in various towns on our way west to pick up more kids. Because our town was in the easternmost part of the state, we had the longest trip of anyone going.

It took until noon to get to the Missouri River, the halfway point. In Fort Pierre, we picked up Faith Taken-Alive, who turned out to be the only Sioux child signed up for the camp. She had a grocery bag full of snacks to share. We all had snacks. We had sleeping bags and suitcases. My friend Andrea and I had laid out our stuff the week before, one outfit for each of the seven days.

At the Missouri River, the terrain changes. Flat prairie land gives way to rolling plains. The farms become ranches. The trees disappear. I could imagine Faith Taken-Alive's ancestors riding there, looking perfectly at home. I looked at her glossy dark head, then out the window again, and felt like a visitor. Faith rode among us, surrounded, outnumbered, provisioned by Frito-Lay.

Crossing the plain translated into an infinite afternoon of unchanging landscape. We sang every song we knew, including "Little Rabbit Foo Foo" and "Ninety-nine Bottles of Beer." Eventually, we took out the tedium on one another. The bus was not air-conditioned, and most of the windows were down, creating a constant roar of wind.

When the strange outline of Bear Butte finally appeared, signaling that the Hills were near, the sudden visual stimulation made us punchy. "Bare butt, bare butt," the boys chanted, as though they were the first in history to think up the joke. How could anyone say "butte" with a straight face anyway.

"Is that your bare butte I see? Why, yes, I believe it is!"

Everyone started thinking up sentences with butte in them. We screamed with laughter. The bus driver seemed to shrink within himself, finally to utterly detach. His spirit, desperate for sanctuary, must roam the sleeping-bear form of Bear Butte yet today.

At last, the bus was ascending. The plains were gone, and we were in a cool forest of tall pines. The light of late afternoon filtered through the trees, making God-shafts that warmed the forest floor. We became focused and alert—not because of the change of scene or because we were recharged by natural beauty, but because we were preparing for a new society. We knew of at least one other bus, scheduled to make its way west across the southern part of the state, bringing kids from bigger towns than ours: Sioux Falls, Yankton, Huron. Who knew how many buses in all would come?

We piled out near the dining hall. We were the last to arrive. Other kids from all over the state had spread out their stuff in the cabins and now hung over the porch rails, watching us. We got our group and chore assignments, found our cabins, and then went to supper. By bedtime, the social hierarchy of the camp was completely in place.

The camp population was two-thirds girls, one-third boys. In the preadolescent sorting that went on, every boy's stock automatically rose. The girls destined for popularity in high school assumed command. The rest of us concentrated on crafts. I spent hours sanding, shellacking, and gluing, making things out of pinecones or pine chips in the craft room. During the afternoon rest period, I sat on my bunk bed and strung love beads, or braided the long strings of colored plastic sold at the canteen. I learned to play tetherball and Ping-Pong. Mostly, I was waiting to go home.

Charlie, being both a boy and one of the older kids, was enjoying a double windfall in the status department. But camp was where Andrea and I got our first inkling of what was in store for us as teenagers: Our schedules would be open, with plenty of evenings free for baking and double solitaire. We would tell each other's fortunes and hope for better times in college. Our mothers would tell us how it was all going to change.

I hid my crush on the boy-god in our group almost immediately, after I found out who else liked him (Janie with the long flaxen ponytail, for one; she told me she meant to be right behind him on the hiking trail at all times). The boy-god had the thick white-blond hair and twinkling blue eyes of Dennis the Menace—or, rather, of the kid who played Dennis on TV. Only he was Dennis grown out of his brattiness into the dreamboat of teen magazines. Two years later, when Andrea and I, in a spasm of idiocy, convinced ourselves to give camp another try, he was there again.

This time he became the property of Debbie Miller, a girl from Arizona whose father had ties to our state. Arizona trumped South Dakota. Debbie's long ash-blond locks, pierced ears, fine legs, and cool sense of entitlement trumped everything else that needed to be trumped. She skipped crafts.

For some reason—maybe my eyes betrayed a hint of helpless worship—Debbie took me up. Visiting in her cabin one day, I listened as she talked about the boy-god: "He'd kiss me and then he'd grin at me," she said. She had a faint, sibilant lisp that sounded sophisticated, especially when she said "kiss." And "Phoenix." She rolled her eyes at the boy-god's performance.

Speechless, I hung on her words. Kissing at our age—twelve or thirteen—was unimaginable enough. But here she was disparaging the most perfect male being in our entire state, implying she could toss him in a minute, like a deuce onto the discard pile. How did a girl get to be so casual toward her good fortune? How could it be so easy to kiss a boy? Or was it that, once you had him, the boy-god was not so much. Surely that could not be true: Debbie was blind to what she had. She looked down on everything, even the camp. She looked down on South Dakota. She said the Black Hills were beautiful; that was why she came. But it sounded rehearsed. Not one junior high kid in a thousand cares about the scenery.

I stopped wondering about Debbie and the boy-god and started wondering about her parents. Who would send such a young girl so far from home? What if she had an emergency, a broken arm or massive loss of blood? She might be lying on the trail to Pactola Dam in her Mexican peasant blouse and hoop earrings, the life draining out of her, and her parents would not know. "Phoenix," she'd murmur, losing consciousness just as her mother, oblivious, was bringing forth a trayful of cocktails in their desert home.

Eventually it came out that Debbie's parents were divorced. The camp was her father's idea of a thing to do with her in the summer, when she was supposed to live with him.

I could not think of anyone in Plainville whose parents were divorced. Divorce was exotic and strange. It enhanced Debbie Miller's stature, partly because of her uncanny genius for making everything that had to do with her seem desirable. Divorce made her wounded, tragic.

"Phoenix." I rolled the word around in my mind all week, imagining myself saying it just the way she would, with extra *s*'s; imagining myself nonchalant in the face of all those highways and stores, bored by the great desert metropolis; the wounded child who was due some great consolation prize.

Another day-long drive in a baking bus took us home. The driver, this time a wiry woman who listened to Country Western songs on a scratchy radio, ran out of gas just before we got to Fort Pierre. We were all stunned: I doubt running out of gas had ever happened to any of us. The driver did not seem too concerned. She looked at us in the rearview mirror. "I thought I could make it," she said. "But bucking that wind, why . . ." She shook her head, resignation in the face of nature.

She got off the bus and started to walk, telling us to stay put. She had not gone very far when a man in a truck pulled over. She spoke to him through the window. "Bucking that wind," we heard her say. He told her to climb in. We sat in the bus on the plains, on the side of the road, with no one, nothing, in sight. The sun beat down on us. We were outraged and also a little thrilled. Would we become a tragedy?

Time uncoiled. Our long day was going to be longer. We

fidgeted, opened more snacks, started to bug one another. We argued about whose seat was whose. It might have been a good time to sing "Kumbaya," but we were all sick of it. At almost any given moment on this interminable camp bus ride, there was someone trying to prod the group into song. But not now. I wondered how long it took for buzzards to circle.

At last, our driver was back. She had been given a lift. In a plastic container, she carried enough gas to get us to town, where we stopped and filled up. The driver, we all agreed, was an idiot who because of poor planning had lengthened the term of our boredom. Not one of us believed the capricious wind of the plains was the culprit. This was a clear-cut case of human error. Life on the prairie was becoming so advanced that we were shedding the fatalism of our forebears. South Dakota was a civilized country, where, if something went wrong, you probably had only yourself to blame.

When at last we arrived home, Charlie and I were not at all prepared for what we found. Our brainy, all-powerful parents, both high school valedictorians, were immobile with despair. As we sat outside on lawn chairs in the dusk, they explained that a man in town was starting a shopping circular to be made up of ads. It would be given away free of charge. The shopper would surely kill the newspapers, kill us; in a town this small, there were just not enough advertising dollars to stretch this far. Already, there were not enough for two newspapers. Leisurely destruction was ambling our way.

I had washed my hair. I was as clean as I had felt in days. At camp I feared the gang showers, which promised certain exposure, and had washed up discreetly and imperfectly. As the week lengthened, I had been torn between dueling forms of shame:

increasingly dirty hair versus being seen naked, which seemed to me intolerable. Now, once again, I met my own family's standard of cleanliness, and my dominant emotion, despite the dire news, was relief.

As our parents laid out the situation, I experienced a peculiar lightness, as if we were a paper doll family. Maybe we would move someplace else and start over, in some town where we were not known. It would be like what happened to the Nelsons.

I did not want to go. No other place could be as familiar as this; no other place could be as real. We would not be real in it: We were part of this place. It was this place, this Dutch colonial house, and the neighborhood of Sixth Street, that told us who we were.

Dad mentioned a paper in Minnesota we might be able to go to. The dark kept coming, and I was grateful. It cloaked my preteen plainness, newly known to me because of the days at camp. Now, home with my family, I did not have to think about that place anymore, about the girls who reigned at the swimming hole in their two-piece suits. The darkness softened, too, our parents' pending failure. I felt their shame merging with mine. Who could compete? What was the system of the world? Why did it make no difference to be good at school? What was wrong with our family?

Shame and fear jostled for ascendancy. Yet another feeling mounted above these—happiness; I was so happy to be home. Our house was solid and inevitable, indistinct from my own consciousness. On one momentous day in the past, it had not burned down. I tried to absorb the news that, very soon, home as I knew it could vanish. But maybe my parents' fears were exaggerated or mistaken. Maybe it would not be as they predicted. Charlie told me later this was quite possible. And if not, there were other places.

But there were no other places for us, I knew. None. In bed

that night my mind worked over the possibilities, the notion of other places. I heard a train sounding its horn as it headed east, disappearing into a night that bucked with impermanence.

Three families, and the families who worked for them, were now trying to till the same small field. It was a tableland of poor soil, insufficient water. Mom and Dad hired two women from out of town to run a subscription drive for our paper. They were grandmotherly and kind. I loved them when I saw them working with their envelopes in the back of the shop. They seemed like two angels who had come to do us a special favor. Maybe there was something wrong with our family. But who could turn down these two sweet ladies?

Dad increased the amount of job printing he did in the back shop—business stationery and forms; newsletters; handbills; anything special that someone wanted printed up. We sold wedding invitations and wedding napkins printed with the couple's name and the date of their big day.

The napkins with mistakes on them we used at home. Sharon and Jerry. Pat and Denny. We were always celebrating some couple or other over our hurried suppers, after which Mom and Dad often went back to the shop. Sometimes, especially if they went with the color scheme Mom was using, the rejected wedding napkins were even brought out for company.

But the most important source of income became the Masons. In summer, all four of us worked to compile the annual proceedings of the Masonic Lodge of North Dakota, breaking the tedium occasionally to announce "so mote it be," a favorite line of the recording secretary. When I was ten, my job was to walk around and around a long rectangular table, collecting all the sections to make one book and then another. The workday was all day until five o'clock. My trips around the table made the undifferentiated prairie outside seem like a land of teeming variety.

The books were glued by hand with a small paintbrush and glue from a can. You spread glue along the spine of the gathered book, carefully placed the heavy paper cover on, and then pushed the spine against the table to seal the glue. It could not drip onto the front or back pages. I was not allowed to glue until I was older.

Charlie and I were paid a small hourly wage. Dad looked us straight in the eye on the first day and said this was our livelihood, and it was important to do it right. When the books were finished, Dad often delivered them himself, driving several hours in the *Herald Advance* van. The books had to be perfectly clean: They were put in boxes and covered with protective paper. It made Dad proud when the Masons said what an excellent job we had done. Once he was a music teacher who could play several instruments. Now he had mastered printing.

We stayed. The *Herald Advance* remained afloat, barely paying for itself. The paper was like some animal you keep for show.

Not long after I graduated from college, I came home to find Mom singing a different tune about work. The paper was now her baby—the thing that made the world go round. Not only that, but Victoria, her rival, was getting on in years. Victoria was going to want to retire one day, maybe to travel. Or maybe she would just putter. Mom's vision that day was deep and absolute. In the end, Plainville would have one paper, and it was going to be the *Herald Advance*.

Yet still she felt so pressed for time. If only she could ease up just a little. If there were only one paper, she could do that.

—Hire help, I said.

—We can't afford to, even if we could find someone. No one would be willing to do the kind of job I do for so little money.

—Do a B job rather than an A job. (I got this from therapy.)

—Not possible. We worked too hard to rebuild our subscription base.

I thought of Grandpa Burges and of Victoria's father, Herbert S. Hatch, duking it out in a contest whose outcome was finally going to be decided through their daughters. Victoria was a good twenty years older than my mother. She had no children to take over if she decided to retire.

She also worshiped her father. Victoria hit sixty-five without so much as pausing in her typing. More time passed. She reached one landmark birthday after another, shrugged off knee problems and faltering eyesight and breast cancer. The *Sun* kept coming, and was rarely without her signature column "Talk of the Town." In time it became clear that Victoria would never quit, not as long as she had breath.

Meanwhile, my parents had moved. The year I finished college and felt my foot fishing for firm land as never before, they left the Sixth Street house and bought a small house of their own. It was their first ever, in a less distinguished neighborhood. Mom refinished all the woodwork and installed chair rails in the dining and living rooms. Upstairs were three tiny bedrooms and the one bath. It was a cheery little place: a dollhouse of a place. Dad, brought up on a farm, always swore he never wanted anything to do with farm life again. Now he was planting strawberries out back and covering them with netting.

All this came about because Grandma Burges had remarried and moved away for a while. Widowed a second time, she came home. She was now Grandma Tait. In the years she had been away, the Sixth Street house had seemed more than ever like our house. When Grandma came back, though, it was clear that it never had been. I felt profoundly cheated.

My parents, nearing their fifties, needed their own place. I understood this, even as I felt betrayed. Now when I came home to visit, it was to the tidy and tastefully redone starter home Mom and Dad inhabited like a pair of newlyweds. I never again stayed in my own room.

In fact, I rarely went to our old house. Grandma rented out the apartment above the garage—where our family had truly started out—to a pleasant elderly couple. She filled the rest of the house with treasures dragged back from estate sales and antique shops. It was as though the home of my childhood had been swallowed whole and had joined the rubble of Pompeii. All that remained were archaeological rambles through memory, and my now-urgent need of a house of my own.

ON THE RANGE

SIR WALTER Raleigh, whose interests went well beyond tobacco, once wrote an essay on romance. "If I had to choose a single characteristic of Romance as the most noteworthy," he wrote, "I think I should choose distance, and should call Romance the magic of Distance."

For an American child of the 1950s, the seminal romance was the West—the West of the cowboys and unfenced terrain, of rangeland where you could ride for days and encounter no one. "The wide-open spaces," everyone said. "Frontierland," Walt Disney said. It is a distinctly American idea. By the 1950s it referred largely to a collective experience of film and TV—that is, to a fantasy.

The wide-open spaces might have been dull but for the enlivening threat of wild animals, outlaws, cattle rustlers, or, especially, an Indian ambush. The Indians of these imaginings generally rode pinto ponies, as though to emphasize that they stood for color and pattern. War paint, beadwork, feathered headdresses—it was all showy, ultimately feminine. The cowboys, in contrast, were drab, mostly brown. Except in the case of an obvious star, such as Roy Rogers, the cowboys' clothes and horses suggested that they were more serious, the kind of can-do people needed to make the country great. We were meant to see that in the true American version, masculinity was dull. The browns of the cowboys were transposed into World War II uniforms without a second thought. Give us any terrain: Our men would blend with it. Whether mending fences or blowing up bridges, our men wore brown.

The West of film and TV could not have been a more perfect emblem of a child's fantasy world. It was a place without rules or authority—just you and your horse (in our case, bike). You did everything outside, even ate there, using your Roy Rogers campfire kit. If a cowboy's world was the open spaces of the West, ours was the streets and yards of Sixth Street. We took cover behind bushes, herded our imaginary cattle toward East Park Avenue, did some ropin' in the churchyard down the block, no cussin' allowed. We did not run but galloped, whipping our horses on, clicking "Giddyup," neighing to get the full range of sound. Figuratively speaking, we were all at home in the saddle.

Every now and then, someone would ride into town on a real horse, go clip-clopping down the streets. Usually it was a country person who wanted to see houses rather than farmland for a change. We heard the sound before we saw the horse and would come running to see. *Please, please take me,* I would pray, paralyzed with longing as horse and rider ambled by. I would watch the animal's regal gait, its languidly switching tail, until horse and rider disappeared from view. No place offered riding lessons; either you had a horse or you did not.

All my horses were toy ones, stabled in shoe boxes in my

bedroom closet. On Saturday mornings, I could hear them nickering with impatience as I woke. My insides would roll over with pleasure. Sometimes I took the horses outside. They thundered down a draw—the place on our corner where bicycles had worn a path from the sidewalk to the street. Mostly, though, the toy-horse terrain was indoors. My horses roamed the high country of the stairs; pastured under Grandma's glass coffee table; escaped mountain lions by traversing the long, perilous ledge above the piano. I knew every inch of that house—its canyons, meadows, and ravines. Thundering herds led by a stallion stampeded routinely across Grandma's kitchen floor.

Sometimes, in the rapt consciousness of play, my toy horses merged with horses I had seen on TV—Champion, Trigger, Silver. I also incorporated a movie horse, a white stallion named Snowfire. He reared up on the screen at the Chateau theater and pawed the cinematic air with his forelegs. But Snowfire was an also-ran compared with Fury. Fury, the black stallion who appeared once a week on TV, was merely the center of the universe. Every Thursday night I watched him wheel and gallop through a black-and-white landscape. I demanded total silence in the room, dreaded that anyone should come by and want to make even a brief remark. Worse, someone might insist on dusting or vacuuming.

"Shhh!" I would hiss, fury personified, if anyone even rustled a piece of paper.

Fury was the perspicacious property of a rancher, but really and truly he belonged to the boy Joey, who loved him the way no grown-up possibly could. Fury was, at heart, a wild stallion. But he hung around because of Joey. In almost every episode, Fury would have to leap the corral fence and gallop off to save the day. The break for freedom was beautiful and satisfying every time.

There were no women to speak of on the show. Fury's world was male and gloriously active. Together, the Newton family had Western-style adventures while making do without a woman's touch. Mr. Newton had to be both dad and mom to Joey, and every once in a while, the show dutifully suggested that this was sad. But, in truth, this world without women, a world uncivilized and unschooled, was deeply appealing. Women in frontier settings were usually only trouble. Either they were frivolous dance-hall girls who distracted the men, or they were plucky wives and daughters who eventually broke down, demanding calico and pianos. *Fury* had none of this.

In the *Fury* years, which were before I became a teenager, I hollowed myself out, made way for the horse. I could be sitting very still, in church or at school, but in spirit I was thundering off, wheeling and rearing, roaming free across the West. I spent hours drawing horses. Most of them I colored black. When, at children's gatherings, we had a choice of cupcake flavors I picked the chocolate over white or pink. When there was a chance to ride a merry-go-round, my eyes searched urgently for a black horse, and I ran for it, prepared to fend off all challengers. On the playground, my feet were hooves. I snorted and whinnied. My nostrils flared. I raced the wind until my lungs were scorched. My tail, a silky banner, swept the ground. I was king, through every change of season, across all the time that I could grasp.

Children who grow up on the prairie spend a lot of time trying to imagine the possibilities. What is out there? How do people live? Their minds are confused museums, cluttered with images from the movies and TV.

Prairie towns basically exist for farmers. You either farm, or, like the Sixth Street people, provide what farmers need: groceries, hardware, clothing, implements. We had a couple of doctors, a few lawyers, an insurance company that grew so that it needed a large brick headquarters on the edge of town. This and the granite quarry and the cheese factory meant that we were better than other prairie towns. We had not just farms but businesses.

Even so, real life was elsewhere; we could tell that from TV. The shows were never about us. The *Andy Griffith Show* came close. Like Americans everywhere, we laughed at the small-town doings in Mayberry, where Andy Griffith played the sheriff. Mayberry, we thought, was really us, even if the writers had erred, and placed their quintessential small town somewhere in the South.

I used to fantasize that somebody famous might come to town. You would walk down to Main Street one afternoon, and there would be Doris Day, looking for a top to go with her skirt. Why not? These people had to be somewhere; what was it about our location that made it so doubtful a famous person would pass through?

Whenever Charlie and I rode our bikes downtown, I kept an eye out. On Main Street we walked our bikes on the sidewalk, looked in the windows. We put the kickstands down and went into Meyer's, the other dime store, across the street from Stemsrud's. We bought candy, including Sputniks, the blue penny gumballs spiked with sugar crystals reminding us that this was the space age.

The owner of the store, Stub Meyer, automatically said "You bet" as he rang up the sale, while "Thank you" hung in our shy throats. He knew us all, and who our parents were. Back out on the sidewalk, our bikes were waiting for us. Why would they not be? If bike locks had been invented by then, the news had not reached us.

I scanned the street, saw nobody famous.

. . .

"Mom, how come nobody famous ever comes here?" I asked once.

She said we were too far away.

From what? I wondered.

Our area did produce one starlet, a girl named Marla Johnson, who changed her name to Lorraine Diamond. Once she came home to visit and to distribute her publicity. Mom fell all over Lorraine Diamond and her husband, Ace, who was also Lorraine Diamond's manager. Marla Johnson looked plain in her high school yearbook picture, but now, as Mom pointed out, "What a dish!"

Lorraine Diamond was apparently in "B" movies, maybe even "C." At any rate, as far as I can recall, her movies never came to town. Lorraine Diamond's career seemed to depend on wearing a bathing suit and showing a lot of leg. When I saw her glossy black-and-white publicity photo, I wondered how her dad felt about all this. He was a farmer and this was his girl Marla. She looked half-naked and ready for some kind of dance-hall-girl trouble.

Mom said I could go on the stage I was so funny. She liked to think of stage names for people. She said I could be May Anders. When she was a girl, Mom said, she thought maybe she would be a movie star when she grew up. She said it as if this might just as easily have happened as what did happen, namely her never leaving her home state or even living anywhere other than her hometown for very long.

While the famous people were staying away, the wind came and went. We were socked in by snow, staggered by temperatures so low they made everything creak, even the air. And then came the mosquitoes in soupy humid weather. All year long, just outside town, the sky kept proposing new colors: dense midnight blue, tangerine, and hot pink; lavender, dove gray, chartreuse. Sometimes it drained itself of every hue, until you thought of skim milk. The sky tones seeped into town, drenching us with color and light, despite the way we had planted elm trees to turn our streets into bowers. Nothing kept out the sky: You could see it at the end of the street, could have walked down and dipped your toe in it. The sky was basic blue. Or it was bruised with thunderheads, a sacred wrap heavy with rain. Nine times out of ten, we noticed it. Our town had not produced a president, poet, sports hero, or marquee idol. But our skies were famous, at least locally.

Mom had one sibling, her little sister Mary. Aunt Mary was addicted to seeing the world and regularly brought back evidence of what was out there beyond the prairie. Grandma's house and our closets were full of souvenirs. We had dolls from Greece, toy soldiers from England. The shelves were crowded with Delftware and Venetian glass.

Once, in her travels, Aunt Mary met Roy Rogers and got his autograph for us. It was addressed to me and Chuck.

"Chuck?" Charlie and I said, looking at each other.

We stared at the scrap of paper. Roy Rogers did not really get us, but at least this showed he was real. He had handwriting with a big angular T (he had signed Trigger's name too). "Be good," it said, "for Roy Rogers, Trigger." Mom put the autograph in a small frame to protect it and to show that we had it.

Our other major autograph was Richard Nixon's. When he was vice president, he made a quick campaign stop at an airport about sixty miles from us. Because Grandma was a big Republican, and our paper supported Republicans, we got to go see him. Mom and

Grandma and Charlie and I, dressed in our good clothes, walked out onto the tarmac to say hello to Richard Nixon.

"Step aside," he told the grown-ups crowding around, "so this boy can get a picture." Everyone backed away. Richard Nixon grinned.

Charlie aimed his Brownie and snapped the shutter. Then Richard Nixon signed his name for us. That was as close as anybody very famous came to our town.

At a holiday gathering not long ago, my sister-in-law talked about Fury. We were in Rhode Island, in the house where my husband grew up, and his whole family was there. The last bites of dessert had been eaten, and we sat with our coffee in the torpor that comes after a feast. Robin said that once, when she was a girl, Fury came to Providence. The real Fury. For some reason, she did not get to go see him, but her friend did. The friend got to pat Fury on the nose.

I could scarcely take this in. The real Fury had been seen. He had been touched by someone who knew someone I knew, who now sat there casually recalling her envy in the dining room of what had become my second family.

Soon, everyone was on to other subjects, but I was adrift. The lace tablecloth disappeared, and the coffee cups, with their dregs of cold decaf. I was making a tour of the arena in Providence, Rhode Island. A thousand children, delirious with love, reached out to touch me. I tossed my coal black mane.

I tried to chart my emotions. It was not envy that I felt, primarily; it was distance—from the being I once was, who, if she had heard this tale, would have been swallowed by a longing so total it would have incinerated the world and every star. The cruelty of my sister-in-law's news would only have been heightened by the offhand way in which it was delivered. The laughter, the drollery that framed the story were part of the intrinsic power of adults— a barbarous power that nullifies childhood desires with irony. With distance.

In childhood I often burned with the determination to remember. "I'm going to remember this," I would vow silently, hotly, brooding over some astounding thing the adults had done— something cryptic, thoughtless, cutting, or unjust. Or I would harbor some sensation I had never heard named, turning it over, seeing it from all sides, silently trying to give it words.

Not only would I remember—I would tell.

No one would escape my report. I would speak as an adult and avenge my childhood self. Fundamentally, I was determined to be, always, who I was—to remain loyal to myself and not change. I loved Fury now, therefore I would love him forever.

Yet here I was, laughing over Robin's story, smiling in retrospective sympathy with her (missing Fury had been crushing), so far from the self I had promised never to betray that this earlier, original self might as well have been on Jupiter.

A story many of us have heard is that the body completely reconstitutes itself every seven years. In that time, supposedly, old cells are completely replaced by new. Thus, by the time you are twenty-one, you move forward without a single cell that participated in the doings of your childhood limbs. If so, are you still the being you were as a child? Are you still, for instance, connected to a certain landscape? Is it impossible to divide your identity from a particular hometown, with its one Main Street pointing arrowlike toward the train tracks? Or must you necessarily depart from who you once were? Are you one self or a series of successive selves?

"But we have memory!" you cry. We have the primitive Proust's madeleine kind, whereby the smell of new tires, for instance, can evoke an entire lost world. But the rest is notoriously unreliable, an ongoing fiction that we create, no matter how fierce our devotion to the past. Rather than being a historical record of one life with its supporting cast, memory is more like a roman à clef.

The narrative of what happened changes—to meet some need, perhaps simply to fill out some idea of a pleasing story. Or one incident gets accidentally spliced to another, seeming to make more sense that way. You will be sitting around the Thanksgiving table: You recount a memory. Another family member says no! That is not how it went; that is not it at all. Then he will supply a version. His version seems familiar, more than familiar. You are stunned to recognize that it is the truth. How can you have gotten it so wrong?

Still, you say, we have recognition—of familiar places, of important people in our lives. It persists from year to year and even deepens as the rest of life changes. But recognition can falter in the fogging illnesses of old age. Less dramatic, you can go to a college reunion and speak pleasantly with someone for half an hour before realizing you knew him, saw him frequently at dinner, shared a class.

I do not know what holiday we were celebrating the day Robin told her Fury story. Prompted by memory, she had dredged up a simple childhood disappointment, one of memory's most basic categories. She had described a gap that could never be filled, a missing experience, a node of perpetual longing that would be part of the narrative of her life for as long as she could recall it. But the longing was gone. What remained was the idea of longing.

The more distant we grow from childhood, the more of a romance it becomes. Meanwhile, it is the child's distance from adults that organizes the day-to-day romance of childhood. Long before we got his autograph, I thought of Roy Rogers as an exemplary man, at once beyond reach and yet in some form out there waiting for me.

When I looked at Roy Rogers on TV, it was the neckerchief that snared me. It was so neatly tied and perfectly fluffed, the scarf of a Boy Scout grown to manhood. Mr. Cleancut. The attractions continued with the eyes. They were deep-set, almost slits, giving Roy Rogers the appearance of always looking into the sun. At the same time, his eyes seemed to lift upward in appeal, like the eyes of a Labrador. They crinkled pleasingly at the edges, evoking gullies.

Roy Rogers was always polite. He was careful around women, children, and animals. Also, he was musical: He could sing and play a guitar. I was aware, too, that he was a Christian, willing to make a very public point about the importance and correctness of his faith. He had a message for kids about where the cowboy code actually came from. I got the idea that the Second Coming could well be Jesus in spurs.

Roy Rogers was chaste. It has been recorded that he never shared a screen kiss with Dale Evans, his TV co-star and real-life spouse.

Above all, Roy Rogers understood the importance of horses. His Saturday morning show made clear that his relationship with Trigger was the main one, that Dale was just around to do laundry and occasionally help move the plot along. This made a deep kind of sense to me.

Like *Fury*, Roy Rogers's TV show emphasized that the ideal terrain was men's terrain. In the drama of power and freedom belonging to the wide-open spaces, men were the main human actors. My identity slid from horse to man and back. I was the sheriff, the range boss, the lone cowpoke on the prairie. Or I was an Indian warrior, riding bareback down Sixth Street, moving with unbelievable stealth among the neighbors' shrubs. I was the glorious chieftain of the Milwaukee Road.

It was simple: I closed the ground between me and the hero of my longing by becoming him.

But what if the hero had actually arrived? What if Roy Rogers, his flesh-and-blood self, had strolled down Main Street one day, perhaps stopped in the Firestone store to purchase a fan belt? What if it had been me, my childhood self rather than Aunt Mary, who had seen him one day and secured his autograph?

Nothing ever happens, I used to brood. No one ever comes here.

Yet Roy Rogers was far more useful to me in dream form than he would have been in person. Imagining him was a necessary type of work, the work a child does to stave off nothingness. In person, Roy Rogers might have shown some unpleasant characteristic. Worse, he might have been handsome and indifferent, signing my scrap of paper with a remote smile and then moving on to the next kid.

I longed for some great and momentous arrival. At the same time, I wanted nothing to change but the seasons. When, perhaps owing to some turn in the light, I thought of the day when I would pack up my toy horses and cease playing with them forever, I would feel immense sadness. It would be the closing of the frontier—a frontier I still regarded as open, infinite, and wholly mine.

At some point during my years on the range, we got a new president, President Kennedy. I did not remember the other. President Kennedy said space was the new frontier. I did not like the idea at all. Astronauts instead of cowboys, John Glenn instead of Roy

Rogers. There were no horses in space. No horizon, no campfires, no coyotes singing to the moon, no wide water to ford. About the only thing that stayed the same was the absence, by and large, of women.

Actually, there was one woman in this new world we were entering. We heard no end of TV and magazine comments on the beautiful and glamorous Jackie, wife of the president. She was ultra-feminine and wore the latest fashions. She had a breathy voice. When other women thought of her, they despaired. Personally, I preferred the long skirts and plain manner of the movies' pioneer women. You might have to be a woman, fine, but you did not have to act like a member of an alien species.

I was in school the day President Kennedy was shot. I cannot remember how we were told. At suppertime, I was massing my herd of mustangs on the blue carpeted stairs, which led from Grandma's living room up to the apartment. The door stood open to the drone of Walter Cronkite. Mom was making supper in the tiny apartment kitchen.

It seemed to me they were going on and on. I understood something important had happened but wished they would stop. They were breaking into my play, breaking up the rangeland with words—with news. I needed quiet so I could hear the whinnying and hoofbeats, the sound of a distant creek running.

Earlier that day, before heading to Dallas, President Kennedy had stopped in Fort Worth. There, someone gave him a cowboy hat to put on. The president felt awkward, did not know what to do. He was an Easterner and clearly thought he would look foolish. He said he would wear the hat later.

I cannot help thinking the cowboy hat might have protected him. Roy Rogers was rarely without his. It was a white hat, which meant he was a good guy. Nothing bad ever happened to him in that hat. But the president was not watching, was not living his true, real life on the range. Our president had his eye on the moon.

Everything got called off. We drove to Grandma Andersen's in Regine and were together in a confused haze of Thanksgiving and national mourning.

"Those poor kids, to lose their dad like that," Grandma kept saying. It made me think of how bad it would be to lose ours. I could see there was an up side to not being famous.

Back home, Grandma Burges took it all in and decided that Lady Bird Johnson had engineered the whole thing so that Lyndon could be president. After all, it did happen in Texas, the Johnsons' home state. When Grandma discussed her conspiracy theory, my skin prickled.

I did not have history clear. How could Dallas look like it did, a modern city with tall buildings, huge crowds, a motorcade passing through, and still be in Texas, home of the range? Roy Rogers's TV show made his life on the range, a cowboy's life, look vaguely up-to-date: His sidekick, Pat Brady, drove a jeep. I figured that meant the range still existed, but what exactly was where?

I knew one thing. Just as no movie stars would come to town, we would not get assassins such as Lee Harvey Oswald. In this way, Plainville was no more connected to history than Regine. We were not important enough for assassins, or for invasions or nuclear attacks. When the teachers led us into the underground tunnel for civil defense drills, they said this was where we would go in case (fat chance) of an emergency.

Okeydokey! We knew there was not going to be any emergency. The tunnel connecting our two school buildings was for the janitors to go through when it got too cold outside—ditto for elementary school students on their way to hot lunch. We cheerfully agreed to come here just in case. Even the teachers felt silly. Before too long, the drills stopped. History happened elsewhere. What we had were growing seasons.

Two years after President Kennedy died, and at the end of the summer, we drove west. Mom and Dad had spent months planning the trip. They arranged for people to take over the paper while we were gone.

"The help" had been drilled, given instructions. Anything that could be done ahead was done.

We were going to visit Dad's brothers. But Mom and Dad said part of the idea of this trip was for us to learn. Thus the most extravagant thing we ever did as a family—three weeks on the road, all the way to California and back—was justified: Learning was a proper excuse for pleasure. As with most prairie families, the circle of calamity and guilt was bred into us. The implicit gamble my family was making was that if the trip was educational, nothing bad would happen to us.

From the moment we got in the car, I was on the lookout for the range. I hoped to see ranches and cowboys, maybe even mustangs. The first day, the landscape we crossed looked mostly like home: flat fields, sky, cattle. We chewed gum and played car games, "Bird, Beast, or Fish" and "I'm Thinking of a Name." We were all excited to be on the way.

We made it to Kansas. In the motel that night I was observed trying to pull the sheets off the double bed I shared with Charlie. Later, when I woke, I was in Mom and Dad's bed.

"What am I doing here?" I said.

Dad told me the whole thing. According to him, I had said, quite distinctly, that I wanted to go home.

I did not remember any of it.

Dad liked Holiday Inns and Best Westerns. We went from one to the next. "I don't like surprises," he said. With a Holiday Inn or Best Western, you knew what you were getting. Every time we picked up our key and opened the door to our room, the place seemed beautiful and luxurious. "Ooh!" we said, checking the empty drawers, removing the sanitary tape from the toilet seat. Charlie and I would go get ice.

Dad was the youngest of three brothers who grew up on a farm in southeastern South Dakota. During college he settled on a crew cut as the thing to do with his hair, and he never changed this, not even in the seventies when some men in town went to sideburns. Dad was not the kind of dad who watched the game or knew scores. He did not golf, fish, or hunt, which made it hard to pick out Father's Day cards for him. Sometimes we just bought the one with a mallard on it anyway.

Dad smoked almost constantly. After work he played the piano, keeping a glass of whiskey and carbonated water within reach. He called the water charged water. Grandma would walk by, mentioning that when you drink, you're killing brain cells. I guess Dad decided that he would take his chances.

He was a shipshape kind of guy. He polished his shoes and cleaned his glasses. Clutter made him anxious. He planned ahead, made lists. For our trip, he had written out what to pack, calculated how far we would go each day. We cut across Texas, bound for New Mexico. An ongoing argument was about whether to stop in the souvenir shop. Charlie and I loved souvenir shops, and so, basically, did Mom, but Dad said it was all junk. It would just be more clutter when we got home.

"Just a few minutes!" we would plead. Usually, he let us.

Charlie and I had brought money we earned from working all summer in the print shop, walking round and round the table as the minutes oozed by. Deciding how to spend it was a sweet agony. Mom wanted me to buy a charm for my bracelet from each state, to remember the trip by. She said I would be glad I had done this. I bought charms of the states of New Mexico, and Arizona. But what I really wanted were those coppery horses with chains in their mouths, Indian dolls, and covered wagon kits. So Mom used her money to buy me some of the charms. I got a galloping pony express rider and, on the way home, an angel like the one on top of the Mormon temple.

Herb Alpert and the Tijuana Brass were on the car radio. They were new, and their music sounded hilarious to us. We turned it up when they came on. Once, Dad woke us at three in the morning so we could cross the desert avoiding the daytime heat. Our car was air-conditioned, but Dad did not want to push his luck. He paid the bill before we went to bed.

When we got up, it seemed exciting, as though we were fleeing danger. If you tried this desert crossing during the day and your car broke down, I figured, you would die panting "Water, water." We pulled out of the motel parking lot in the dark, while everyone else was still sleeping. They did not have the wise foresight of our family. Herb Alpert was on the radio playing "Whipped Cream" as we headed west, pursued by dawn. By the time the sun got to us, the desert was safely past, and we were ready for breakfast.

. . .

I continued to look for the range. Hour by hour I watched for roundups and wild stallions. We did not see them. So far the only cowboys we had seen were in wax museums. We saw all the legendary figures of the West: Wyatt Earp, Calamity Jane, Buffalo Bill.

Charlie and I loved wax museums—the cool dark of them, the dreamy staring figures. Each character was allotted a small personal stage. Some moment from the life was suggested, as though that moment wrapped up the person. Strolling past the wax figures, we reviewed the national mythology, while taking time to appreciate all the hard work that had gone into this. On one figure, we would applaud the mustache. On another, it would be the fancy buckskin jacket or tooled-leather boots. Sometimes we would praise the details in the setting: "Look at the whiskey bottle," someone would say. We admired the special lighting that signified high noon.

When we came out of the wax museum into the hot glare of August, I would instantly feel sad. Here was the wide earth again, the bright blue sky with its roaming buffalo clouds. Where to? What next?

No wonder people created legends, built wax tributes, thought up dark rooms that other people would pay money to enter. The world could feel empty, and you never knew when the feeling might hit you.

We did not see a real cowboy, but we did see an Indian. As we drove along through scrubland in the Southwest, we came upon a pup tent propped by the side of the highway. It turned out to be one of a few we would encounter. In it was a Navajo boy in something approximating native dress. He was advertising that you could have your picture taken with him for fifty cents.

To my embarrassment, we stopped and got out. No one else was around; no buildings or cars were in sight. You could not tell where this boy lived, where he went home to at the end of the day.

He eyed us calmly. "Got any comic books?" he said.

Charlie and I shook our heads no.

"Any Fritos?"

We shook our heads again. Then we lined up against the Southwestern landscape, with cactus bounding off into infinity, and had our picture taken with the real Indian boy.

We stopped at the Painted Desert, the Petrified Forest, the Grand Canyon. We looked. There that is, we said. We were not hikers or rock hounds or nature lovers. From a parking area we gazed down into the Grand Canyon, an infinite regress of stripes, brick-colored and purple, the sun hammering it in places into sheets of gold. Vast vastness, I thought. When you looked as far down as you could see, your stomach bounced, as if you had driven a good thousand miles before realizing you had left the iron on back home. People all around us peered into the canyon and said nothing. Finally what you noticed was the sky again. Nothing, not even the Grand Canyon, dwarfed the Western sky. Knowing that it was futile, everyone tried to take pictures anyway.

"Well," Dad said at last, careful not to rush anyone. "Should we go?"

No wild stallions. No cowboys twirling lariats or driving a herd of cows to Abilene. No one wielding a branding iron, a six-shooter, a set of hobbles. I stared out the window, and made up my own.

. . .

The closer we got to California, the more we wondered about the ocean. We knew lakes but not oceans, boats but not ships. How deep would the ocean be? How high the waves? What did salt water feel like?

Our ocean thoughts were soon crowded out by traffic. The lanes of the road multiplied. We passed highway strip after highway strip, a ceaseless panorama of restaurants, stores, and offices. You could never see the center of anything. California was a maze, with palm trees and McDonald's hamburger places. I did not see how it was possible, amid this infinite tangle, to locate the one house that was Uncle Elton's. But as if drawing a necessary ace from the deck, Dad at length pulled up in front of the correct bungalow.

We got out of the car, stiff from hours of riding, glowing with the feat of our arrival. Here we were, all the way from South Dakota. Our relatives rushed to bring us something cold to drink, to help carry our stuff in, to get us settled for a good visit.

Uncle Elton and Aunt Ruby had three children. Steve and Connie were older than we were, teenagers now, and thus qualified for automatic veneration. Mark was younger, a little boy with delicate feelings and a close-shaved blond head. His sister teased him and told him he looked like an onion. All three played the piano like pros, the result of strict practice schedules laid like wire grids across their blossoming natural talent. I envied them and also was glad I was not them. Along with having to practice, they had to be in church a lot.

Uncle Elton and Uncle Dale—products of the same farm Dad grew up on—had both moved their families out to Riverside from Sioux City, Iowa. They loved California and said they would never go back. They bragged about the weather, the fruit you could just pluck from trees anytime. I thought of how our cousins had no snow at Christmas and felt sorry for them. What did they do? Decorate a palm tree? The real Christmas had snow. If you moved here you gave that up. You might still open presents, but it would feel like the fake ritual of a serviceman's family posted overseas.

I tried to connect Uncle Elton and Uncle Dale with a large picture Grandma Andersen had of the two of them together in their Navy uniforms. In the picture they looked young and shiny, coated with sweetness. Dad was the baby in the family and completely missed the war. But while his brothers sailed the ocean, he scanned the prairie skies for enemy aircraft. He had memorized their silhouettes and was ready for the thing that never came.

None of the brothers wanted to farm. They all wanted town jobs. Growing up, they had done enough farm chores to satisfy them for a lifetime. Dad remembered the plow horses rolling around in the dirt at the end of the day because they were so glad to get the harness off their backs. The Andersen brothers envisioned town jobs as providing the same relief.

Like many farmers, Grandpa had not been lucky. He lost his land during the Depression and for a while reported to assorted work details thought up by the government—drainage projects and such. When he got back to farming, he rented land. But his sons all saw how thankless it was—how wearing on body and soul.

Still, home, for Dad's brothers, was farm country—the place we had just driven so far from. I guessed that when they got to California, they had had to figure out a way to hold the Midwest in and keep the new place out. I could see the problem: It was all around Uncle Elton's house. Endless places to go, things to do, stuff to buy. You would have to push so hard against it all to finish your homework, to remember God. Also, you could not know everybody here, so why know anybody? In our town, you could run through all the possibilities and figure out who you liked best. Finding a friend had ultimate rather than arbitrary meaning.

I sensed something caged about our California cousins. The cage was built out of love and fear. Back home, we did not need to be caged. The town limited what there was to do and hope for, to get mixed up in, and so the parents did not need to bother setting limits. They could do an indifferent job, and the town would take care of the rest.

For instance, down at the movie theater, Mr. DeBoer would call your parents and tell them to come and get you if you acted up during the show. Mr. Cameron, the high school principal, dragged rebellious boys into the office and, with some, insisted that they join the service after graduating—and, by golly, they were going to graduate. The ones that joined the service came back to thank Mr. Cameron for straightening them out.

But who would keep track of the boys in such a big and confusing place as California? In California, the weather invited people to keep doors and windows open all the time. The outside beckoned. But our cousins could not really go anywhere, I saw, not without a ride. Down the block it was just more houses and beyond that still more. We were the normal ones, I was pretty sure; we came from a real town with farms all around it. Having a lemon tree in your backyard did not make up for the fact that you were in exile.

On TV, we saw clouds of smoke, pillars of fire. People were running, fighting, and shouting. The police came with clubs and tear gas. How far away, exactly, was Watts? I asked Dad if the fighting would come to where we were. He said no, that it was in Los Angeles, which was far away from Riverside. He looked it up on a map.

The adults said not to worry. But the rioting went on, day after day. In the morning Charlie and I would rise from our bedrolls on the floor, and the TV would show the aftermath of the night before. When we were in the car, the men kept track of the Watts riot on the radio. One day it was announced that rioting had broken out in San Bernardino, which was closer to Uncle Elton's. What if we got lost and drove into San Bernardino by accident? We could be dragged from our car like other white people this had happened to. We could be beaten up and killed.

"Dad?" Mark said, his eyes blinking. "Why don't they bomb them?" He sounded sweet and innocent, like the kid on *The Rifleman* (another TV Western with an absent mom). *"Paaw? Why don't they bomb 'em?" Lucas McCain's eyes narrow with flinty purpose; he cocks his rifle.*

The adults looked at the TV and shook their heads. Why were the Negroes doing this? I felt ashamed for the rioters. They were making themselves look bad. They were burning their own neighborhood, their own stores. It did not make any sense. They were tearing apart their home.

Every day, while the National Guard tried to bring order to southwestern Los Angeles, we kept having our vacation. We had planned and saved for it for so long. We had the chicken dinner at Knotts Berry Farm, which came with giblet gravy and mashed potatoes. Mom and Charlie and I went on a ride through a fake mine. It was exciting and scary, with a big splash of water at the end.

Our visit to the ocean was so quick I barely remember it. "Just run and stick your toe in," Mom said, "so you can say you've touched the Pacific Ocean." We had picked some built-up spot, left the car, scampered down, plunged a foot in. Now what? Dad was ready to go. The drying salt water left a film.

When we got back to Uncle Elton's, we watched the news and saw how the day had gone in Watts. Night was the time to worry. That was when it started up again, and maybe could spread. Because of movies I knew to believe in the U.S. cavalry. In this case, the cavalry was the National Guard and the police. Order always triumphed. Steve and Connie and Mark were not allowed to stop practicing the piano just because there was rioting in Watts.

Disneyland was the star at the top of the tree—the culmination of our trip. We were going to spend a whole day, and at last the day came. Again we were on the freeway: more freeway driving in California's happy-all-the-time weather while listening to the riot report, and then we were parking in a lot bigger than our town. We bought passes for the day.

We could not stop saying how clean everything was. We got fresh orange juice from a spotless little stand, where a young woman with blond hair was as nice to us as anyone from home would have been. Maybe nicer.

All the employees are helpful and friendly, Dad said. They really do it right.

He approved of Disneyland in a global way. To Dad, one of the worst things you could have was a surly employee. The person he most approved of in the world was a pleasant person, even just to run into on Main Street. The person did not necessarily have to be waiting on you. Whenever this idea of his came out, I felt bad, the way I did sometimes when I watched Disney shows. Except for the villains, the characters in these shows were always so good.

I knew that I had more badness in me, and the sense of comparison seemed to bring it out. Cousin Mark was cute and sweet and good. Sometimes I wanted to bean him for that reason alone.

At Disneyland we walked down a broad spotless avenue to the castle of Fantasyland, which looked just the way it did on TV. There was also an old-fashioned Main Street, with ice cream parlors and fancy streetlights. It was way more appealing than our Main Street back home: Why did our Main Street not look the way a Main Street was supposed to look? This showed it could be done.

Mom and Charlie and I rode the monorail, which was so safe and smooth it was practically no fun. Dad did not like rides. He chose to wait for us. "You won't even go on the *monorail?*" Charlie and I moaned. What a chicken. Dad did not like crowds or things he could not get out of quickly. At concerts and in church, which he rarely attended, he took an aisle seat. He said it was claustrophobia.

After the monorail, all four of us went into a theater where the lights went down, and a model of Abraham Lincoln gave a whole speech. He seemed real, gesturing and cocking his head, his eyes sweeping the crowd for agreement.

Our family agreed with him so much we had chills. There was music and patriotic imagery. But most of the effect came from Abe Lincoln talking, slowly and deliberately, in front of a crimson curtain. This was a great country, he said, and we were noble people. I was so sure he was right I wanted to cry.

When the lights came up and it was time to leave the theater, our minds flew to the essence of the spell. How did they do that? we all wanted to know. Was it batteries? Hidden wires? Was the figure technically a robot? Whatever it was, it was really good. It was outstanding. Americans sure knew how to do things. You would not find something like this in, say, Brazil.

Toward evening a huge crowd gathered to hear Duke Ellington play. I did not know who he was, but I got the message. Although he was a Negro, Duke Ellington was not breaking store windows in Watts. He was here making music. He had gone out and gotten a job. It was really very simple in our land of opportunity, the land mechanical Abe Lincoln had just told us about.

I did not know it, but only a few months before, Duke Ellington had been the subject of angry conversations in New York. For the second year in a row no Pulitzer Prize in music would be given. The music jury had unanimously recommended a citation for Duke Ellington—the durable Duke Ellington, who had emerged in the 1920s as one of the great jazz band leaders, then fallen into years of playing last sets to empty rooms, and kept going all the same. Duke Ellington, for whom the greatest instrument was not a trumpet or tenor saxophone, but the whole band—a band that had held together longer than any other and had risen again one unexpected evening in Newport in 1956.

That night the band members, missing four sidemen, were pulled off the stage and left to stew in a tent for three hours, after which their pent-up music exploded. The rich cats swarming on the lawn dug it—would not, in fact, let the Duke Ellington band leave the stage. Not long afterward, and only a few months before the rioting in Watts, the Pulitzer board rejected the recommendation of its own music jury. When the board declined to honor Duke Ellington, two of the three jury members resigned in protest.

What was it to Duke Ellington? As I was there to see, he went on playing. It would be another thirty years—long after he was dead—before any Pulitzer board would honor Duke Ellington. By then it would have dawned on Americans what we had here— merely a new art form, a community of sound built and guided by a black man, whose inspirations skated from old slave songs to Debussy. More prosaically, by then, my own innocence of racial issues would have vanished.

One time, a trombonist asked Ellington to tell him where the chord changes would be in a song they were going to play.

"Chord changes?" said Ellington, giving him a look. "Listen, Sweetie!"

Otherwise what did they have? If they could not hear each other, what did they have? Once upon a time, my family sat and listened to Duke Ellington as evening came to Disneyland, the cleanest and most orderly place in the world.

We were just as happy to leave California. With every mile, we were putting Watts farther behind, getting safer and safer, casting off an obscure sense of guilt. We stayed at the Sands, in Las Vegas. One night cost fifty dollars, the most we had ever heard of for a hotel room. Mom and Dad went to a late floor show, no kids allowed. Charlie and I stayed in the room. We watched TV and got ice.

In the morning, Las Vegas looked prim and well meaning, as all places do. We had breakfast and drove on. Next came the Great Salt Lake, the miracle of the seagulls who saved all the Mormons, and a tour of the Beehive House, where Brigham Young kept I don't know how many wives, in room after room. I set my face in an expression of disapproval and maintained it through the whole tour. My disapproval ran from South Dakota through mechanical Abe Lincoln to me, an American child who knew what was right. One man, one wife.

Because we were considered infidels, our family was not allowed into the great temple itself. We listened to the Mormon

Tabernacle Choir practice and saw a film about Mormonism, which showed Mormons in white robes meeting their loved ones after they died. Salt Lake City was almost as clean and orderly as Disneyland. Crime was rare. For sure no one would riot. But I could not wait to get out of there. Obedience was the whole story. Men obeyed God. Women obeyed men. Then came the children. I imagined a life of church and self-denial like my cousins'.

We headed for the Rocky Mountains. Mountains! Land rising up! I was astounded as our car edged around the blasted face of the rock, taking us higher and higher. To a prairie child, mountains are so unlikely they appear manmade—an enormous set perhaps, courtesy of Disney. Mom took out the movie camera and filmed the view, along with Dad's knuckles on the wheel. He did not like this scenic drive. The guardrails looked flimsy. We could go plunging over the side, whipping past evergreens stubbornly trying to grow.

I watched for bears. A grizzly could rip your limbs off and then your head. It was best to stay in the car. Also, on TV, Smokey the Bear had warned us about forest fires (us, in the treeless heart of the treeless prairie). We knew not to carelessly toss a lit match. I kept an eye on Dad's cigarettes, which he was smoking one after another as we spiraled on up. Luckily, we were not campers. We had no campfire plans whatsoever. We were going to get out of this blameless.

It all culminated in our standing in a ring with hundreds of others, waiting for Old Faithful to gush in a high fountain, which it did. The license plates in the parking lot were from every state you could think of. Pennsylvania, Arizona, Ohio, New Jersey. Even Alaska. Everyone applauded the geyser when it was done. Then off we all trooped to the gift shop.

By then I had a huge boil on my face. Mom and Dad figured it had to do with my diet, which since the trip began was mainly fried chicken, hash browns, and orange pop. They bought me some ointment to put on at bedtime. I woke with one side of my face black and crusty with dried goo. We were in a cabin in Wyoming, which we stayed in because we could not get a Holiday Inn. After I picked the goo off my face, we went for pancakes and sausages at a place where you ate inside a teepee. It was chilly, and the hot pancakes tasted good. Mom and Dad said this part of the trip was a pleasant surprise, a highlight even.

I was still looking for cowboys and wild horses—for the open range. The closer we came to South Dakota, the more I realized I was not going to see it. We were going home to a place where cows stayed in fenced pastures, where keeping horses had become beside the point. We crossed the rolling plains of western South Dakota. Then the familiar barns and silos of the east-river prairie came into view. Dad said how nice it was to see the high sky again—big sky—and I stared at the horizon and did not know what he meant. Land and sky, sky and land. What was so different?

Then we were in our driveway, and I was unloading my Tinkerbell doll and other souvenirs. In the fall I took my seat at school, the only kid in my fifth-grade class to have ever seen Disneyland, and incidentally the Pacific Ocean. I had to be careful not to brag.

Edmund G. Brown, the governor of California, had set up a study commission on Watts, and it reported back shortly before Christmas: Negroes had migrated to Los Angeles from the south, the commission said, and encountered frustration. Three "aggravating events" fueled their discontent: the repeal of California's fair housing act, federal anti-poverty programs that did not deliver as promised, and "the angry exhortations of civil rights leaders." Other than that, "what happened was an explosion—a formless, quite senseless, all but hopeless violent protest."

I doubt I heard about it. I shut out Watts and history, which somehow did not concern us here in the country's well-ordered and sensible middle. I fastened myself to the seasons, to the eternal life of our town. On the living room floor, I returned thankfully to the range.

THE BETHEL

ON A summer night when Mom could see I was old enough, she told me the facts about babies. She told me what would be happening, shortly, to my body. We were in the apartment above the garage together, and the windows were open. I could hear the neighborhood kids running in one of the games we loved, the slap of their tennis shoes on Sixth Street.

I could barely breathe. I felt I could not move. How could I continue my excellent work as an Indian scout, crawling silently through the bushes, if I was going to have breasts? I felt infinite shame, for myself and for our whole human species. Everything Mom was saying was the worst news I had ever heard. Outside, someone kicked the can, which meant all the prisoners could go free. The can clattered across the street, and I could hear kids running fast and hard for freedom. I sat frozen, not wanting to have a body, not wanting anyone to see me or my body with its disgusting potential. Eventually, I did go outside, but my movements were stiff and slow. The darkness, usually welcoming, did not conceal a thing.

. . .

Time passed. It passes. We never know how much or how long, only the successive places where it pins our being to existence. The closet, for instance. How well I remember my closet in the Dutch Colonial on Sixth Street. The shoe boxes inside the closet. At some point after that summer night or maybe at the exact moment Mom said "babies," my horses became pieces of plastic shaped like horses. They stayed in their boxes in the closet. Palominos, chestnuts, bays, and Appaloosas: Henceforth, they did not make a sound.

I went forward. I had the great illusion of going forward. Time was not a circle consisting of the seasons but an arrow heading toward an unrevealed perfection. Or was it heading toward a kind of prison, a job and children, endless cooking, with no time to think? At certain moments it seemed the arrow pointed straight to God and that nearly everything that happened on Earth was simply a form of cosmic detour.

For some people, a very big detour ran through Omaha Beach. Another ran through just plain Omaha, Nebraska. In 1804 Lewis and Clark camped on a plateau overlooking the Missouri River, in the place that would become Omaha. In 1825 an Indian trading post was established there, but for years visitors were few. The human tide came in 1854 when the Nebraska Territory opened for settlement. Omaha came to be, with railroads and stockyards, meat packing and a telegraph link to San Francisco. The Mormons came and the Mormons went. Omaha endured the slight. By 1880 it was home to more than thirty thousand people.

Into this river plateau bustle, with its sweet mournful vistas, and more than the usual dread of nothing-to-do, came a child named Ethel T. Wead. Her philosophy might have been anything, except that fate dealt her mother, Elizabeth D. Wead, a tricky hand: She was widowed and forced to raise her children alone in what was still a frontier town. Whatever happened must have scared young Ethel, for in 1920 after she married Dr. William H. Mick, she founded an organization for girls, to prepare them for a life of all-but-guaranteed calamity. The Order of Job's Daughters, as it was called, was for budding females who had family ties to the Masons. Mrs. Mick, after some thought, evidently decided that it was all well and good to talk about Jesus, but what girls really needed to gird them for the fight was a good dousing in the Book of Job.

Job, of course, is the Ur-story of unexplained suffering. Satan is sent by God to test Job, a wealthy but pious man. He destroys Job's flocks and servants, collapses a house on his sons, and basically subjects him to every possible plague, including boils. Yet Job does not lose his faith in God, and in the end prosperity is restored to him.

Ethel T. Wead Mick especially liked the line "In all the land, none were so fair as the daughters of Job," which was something her mother liked to spout. All her daughters, Elizabeth Wead said, should strive to be like the daughters of Job. So the loyal Ethel founded her order, to encourage girls to be what she imagined her mother meant. They should be reverent, true, patient, and faithful. And they should of course be fair, which meant that even in the land of the stockyards, on the dun-colored shoulders of the Missouri, it was important for a girl to look good.

My friend Meg, the great-granddaughter of the eminent agricultural researcher Niels Ebbesen Hansen, could not wait to join Job's Daughters. She liked all the things about growing up, so Job's Daughters was made for her. Even if you were still only in junior high, in Job's Daughters you got to be around high school girls.

Time's arrow was made for Meg, but I glowered in my corner. What would growing up get me if it was only about turning into a woman? I looked to Meg for clues, tried to watch how she approached everything. But it was harder now. Meg's family had moved several blocks away to a brand-new house on one of the newer streets. The new streets and houses were on the edge of town, not in the heart of it the way Sixth Street was.

I kept forgetting to go over there. Or when I tried to go, Meg had a million new friends hanging around, especially boys. They wore shapeless green army jackets and said little and were subject to sudden collective bursts of hysterical laughter. Meg and I could not talk the way we used to, when it was just us presiding over our Barbies. Meg had new friends from the new neighborhood, and it was hard to get on her schedule. We saw each other regularly, though, at Job's Daughter meetings.

The masonic hall, when the Daughters of Job inhabited it, was officially called the bethel. It had been constructed years before above a Main Street storefront, and the wooden staircase leading up to it was easily the longest and most exhausting staircase in town. The hall itself was unusually long and narrow, with a dais and three thronelike chairs at one end and benches along the sides. At the other end, two sets of tall double doors opened onto the room. From one you could march in, and from the other out.

Just outside the meeting room was a mammoth furnace that whooshed on and off, a powder room, and a small reception area with a kitchen and closet. The whole place smelled of ancient radiators, worn linoleum, old candle wax, plastic tablecloths, plastic doilies, and plastic drawer liners growing sticky in the drawers. The air bore leftover traces of scented powder and perfume and coffee made in large urns. And in the bathroom, though it was faithfully kept clean, I seemed to smell dried menstrual blood. I imagined it accumulating in layers over years going back to the time when Ethel T. Wead was a girl; perhaps it was the minerals in our hard water that had fixed this odor just so.

Although Grandpa Burges had been one, the Masons were no longer active in our town. Gradually the masonic temple had become a women's place, used by members of the Eastern Star (the women's auxiliary group) and by us, the newest South Dakota chapter of the International Order of Job's Daughters.

We numbered around twenty. The organization was highly structured, with multiple offices. A small booklet told us how to run meetings, which prayers to say, which songs to sing. *"Behold, behold: We are the daughters of Job."* That was one. The overall objective was for us to be versed in the story of Job, which was periodically recited (as condensed and rewritten by Mrs. Mick) in five parts by five girls. Life was suffering, we took turns sweetly explaining—inexplicable, relentless suffering. Take the case of this one pious man, God's humble servant Job. He was afflicted, and the heavens seemed to give no answer. Yet there is one. Remain faithful, have patience, and you will receive your reward.

I was fairly suspicious of the subtext. The organization had been founded when Grandma Burges was a girl, and her lack of options in life was something I was instructed in from day one. Like a packhorse, I carried around Grandma's lack of options, also Mom's unfortunate necessity to work, the big unifying theme being that women could not get what they wanted. Yet as far as I knew, the masonic organization for young men, DeMolay (which our town did not offer) was not built around a tale of suffering. Apparently, as the master Masons who gave us heritage saw it, suffering was the lot of women. Maybe they were thinking of our periods and childbirth. The sooner we got used to the idea that suffering was coming, the more readily we would accept the harness. With the help of that fine woman Ethel T. Wead Mick, the Masons were planting a little seed with the young ladies of America. In our chapter, we were fertile ground all right, but not for the message of suffering. Behold, we saw ourselves quite clearly. Our purpose, our sole reason for being, was as strong and singular as a maypole—to sponsor dances at the city aud.

Every month under new business, the older girls would offer the names of bands that they had heard were good. Someone would volunteer to do the booking, someone else to reserve the old city auditorium, another to put up the posters. We also had to hire a cop, who would stand there and frown in an official attempt to ward off underage drinking and an unofficial one to forestall premature sexual relations.

The bands were all rock bands, made up exclusively of guys with long hair or beards or both. We danced in the dark to music so loud that our ears still rang the next morning in church. The feelings of the city aud neighbors were a perpetual issue. "Purple Haze" would shake the Methodist parsonage across the street. The daughters of Job had introduced amplifiers and electric guitars to our town, and this brought up new quality of life concerns. Sometimes the cop or the bethel guardian or one of the Job officers would go up onto the stage and say the volume had to come down because of complaints. For a while, the band would try to comply. It was all loud though. The only variations were loud or louder.

Also introduced to our town by Job's Daughters, or so it seemed to me, were the sweaty palms and stiff circular rocking à deux known as slow dances. Likewise, it was the fairest in the land who first posed the question of what to do during a drum solo.

You could not really dance to it, so did you stand there rhythmically moving your head, or did you go out to the hall for a drink of water? The choice depended on how cool you felt. I went out for water.

The Job's Daughters' treasury bloomed. We had cash on hand. Receipts outstripped debts by a satisfying margin. The treasurer, Mary Sawrey, was a large and serious girl who spoke softly when she read out the numbers. Like the rest of us, she wore a white cotton robe with white braid crisscrossed over her heart. The two ends of the braid wrapped around the back and came forward again to be tied in front at the waist. The tasseled ends hung nearly to the floor. Since our meetings took place mostly during the chilly months of the school year, the thin fabric of our robes provided inadequate warmth. Their draping and full length reminded us we might be brides one day, if we did not first succumb to exposure. When bored or cold, we twirled the long ends of our tassels as though they were twin jump ropes. Some of us became quite skilled and could bring the pair closer and closer together until, with one hand, we were twirling them both in opposing concentric circles.

"Girls. Don't twirl your tassels," our adult adviser (the bethel guardian) would admonish. And we would stop for a while, vaguely aware that our praxis shared something with the stripper's art.

For that matter, we did a number of burlesques on the idea of the feminine, the good-girl image proffered to us by Ethel T. Wead Mick and seconded by the master Masons. Susan, slightly bow-legged, trundled along in the marches exaggeratedly chewing gum on one side of her mouth, in homage to some tough girl ideal. Shirley and Debbie called each other Big Shirl and Big Deb, as though they were gangster molls or dames stuck in prison. And several of us imitated the dirty old man from the TV show *Laugh-In* as we dressed and undressed in the dim curtained-off area behind the dais. We edged near one another in our slips: *"Do you believe in the hereafter? Then you know what I'm here after. Ha!"*

White dress shoes were required. But no one wanted to spend money on a good pair just to wear to a Job's Daughters meeting, so we had a collection of castoffs, some from rummage sales, others left behind by girls who had graduated. The white-shoe box, a tall cardboard container in which our footwear was stored, held some of the most hideous styles ever perpetrated on U.S. females. The shoes had chunky heels or tiny spiked ones, T-straps or pointed toes, garish buckles, outlandish bows. Often they were too big, and we glided into the hall as though on skis. The delicate loveliness suggested by our official Job's Daughter robes was effectively canceled by our Minnie Mouse shoes.

I studied the older girls for how to be. The funnier and raunchier the girl, the more protean she was. Susan and Shirley both had a sophisticated sense of style and a knack for handling hair and makeup. When they dressed for an event, they could make the school's prettiest cheerleader look irredeemably homespun. People in town still talk about Susan's wedding, a Christmastime affair at which she stepped into the church looking like a 1940s film star, in a column of white satin she had designed herself. Shirley convincingly played the ingenue in a number of local plays, in musicals filling the auditorium with a May-wine soprano that made everyone think she would be a professional one day. Yet both of them were gross-out queens in full command of rumbling burps and an ever-expanding repertoire of crude jokes.

We would truly have been the despair of Mrs. Mick had our chapter not featured so much musical talent. Shirley, Susan, a half dozen others—they simply could not help themselves, no matter how smarmy the hymn. In the closing ceremony, we knelt in a cross formation, and with the lights low sang "Nearer My God to Thee." The sound was full, the harmony unwavering. Through most of the meeting, we shivered in our robes, hugged ourselves to keep warm. But hearing one another's voices, we concentrated on melting into the folds of the hymn. We briefly forgot about the cold. Imitating reverence, we became reverent.

In those days I did not know anything about the Ku Klux Klan. It was years before I realized that a discerning outsider, stumbling on this group of white-robed girls amid all their Christian paraphernalia, in a farming community taken almost wholly from German and Scandinavian stock, might get the wrong idea— might feel, even, a gust of alarm. But no one would have appreciated the gulf between this misapprehension and our reality more than we. Far from practicing evil, we were a public service organization. We had prestige. We were the Daughters of Job, in dorky white shoes, and we brought the rock bands to town.

If a boy liked you, you found out at the Job's Daughter dance. You found out in a slow dance what it was like to touch a boy and have him touch you. You watched the other girls: how they moved, how they smiled. And of course how they dressed. We learned to value wool for winter as a status fabric. Good wool pants and good wool skirts: A-line skirts, dirndl skirts, pleated skirts, kilts with a large gold diaper pin to keep them from flapping open, wool jumpers and wool sweaters.

Katherine Spears—with blue eyes, an upturned nose, and perfect white teeth—was the best dancer in the school. But she never had an adequate partner until the foreign exchange student from Germany came. He was Rudy Gerhard, and the night he partnered

Katherine at a Job's Daughter dance, no one could stop watching them. For most of us in those days, dancing was a side-by-side form of rhythmic convulsions, but Rudy and Katherine danced in each other's arms, sweeping across the floor and twirling in unison. Katherine's hair, brushed back from her face, was piled high on the back of her head and miraculously held its place no matter what she did. She wore stockings and shoes with a heel; she wore a wool outfit. It made her too warm. When she and Rudy came out to the hall for water, both were panting and their color was up. They were having a great time, as in the fantasy of what youth is supposed to be like. Katherine, everyone knew, was only in it for the dancing, although she liked Rudy well enough. It showed how hard finding true love was going to be, if there was no one for Katherine Spears.

In the meantime, a girl needed wool skirts and wool sweaters, and at least one pair of good wool pants. We all had blue jeans, but they were not the attire of choice for public events. And anyway, for girls, they were barred in school—as were pants in general until my senior year. The administration kept watch over our skirt lengths and cracked down from time to time when the skirts were considered too short. If judged in error, we could be sent home to change. If that was not possible, we were told that the offending garment was herein and henceforth banned from the sacred premises of our school. Otherwise, unspecified wrath, penalties, etc., would rain upon our wanton heads.

The wardrobe that arose from this setting, the pretty smocks and tailored wool pants that I sewed for myself, turned out to be profoundly wrong, a few years later, for college; there, painters' pants and crewneck sweaters were the uniform of choice. I do not remember how I got rid of the cheery pink pantsuit I had once so loved, but I did it after wearing it to Lit 141 one day. As I sat taking notes, the professor's eyes, with a kind of question in them, lingered on me just slightly too long. I felt the slow spread of what I had formerly thought of merely as blushing, and now knew to call an epiphany, through my complete person. I slithered back to my room in mortification and did not ever wear my pink pantsuit again.

Home is partly a matter of how we dress. Do the eyes of others approve? Do we look sufficiently like them? The dress code changes from place to place, from year to year, until in the end you appreciate its arbitrariness and become too exhausted or simply unwilling to keep up. After that, you stop seeing yourself—do not know what you look like. The moments in which a woman feels most beautiful are also those in which she feels most at home in the world. I suspect even for the very beautiful, only a handful of such moments may come. (Once, a few years before she became Miss South Dakota, I saw Katherine Spears behold her own faultless face in a mirror and frown.)

But the reverse is also true. When a woman feels at home in the world, she is beautiful. Think of the rare woman you have met who is at peace with her surroundings. She has no compelling need to fix the place up or herself either. Without fanfare, she merely does the necessary work. When a visitor arrives, she pauses, shares, listens. The visitor goes away moved, wondering what her secret is. The visitor fears that she herself has not lived. I felt this sometimes when I visited Meg's new house—a modern place with brand-new carpeting and a huge kitchen—in which Meg at last had her much-longed-for room of her own. Meg's desires, however, were not the reason for the move. This house had no stairs, and its proportions accommodated a wheelchair. Every kid on Sixth Street knew about multiple sclerosis because Meg's mother had it. First she was stumbling a bit and making mysterious, inconclusive visits to out-of-town doctors. Then came a cane, a walker, a wheelchair. No one could remember the last time she had been upstairs in the house on Sixth Street, the house she loved. And so the family moved.

Pretty soon, I could not remember Meg's mother walking. It seemed she had always been in a wheelchair. In my mind, the last time she walked I did not see but felt: It was the time of the fire, when she picked me up and carried me home.

When I saw her in the new house calmly folding laundry or settling some family dispute, I felt transfixed by her at-homeness. Not one of us in Job's Daughters really needed to be hammered by the idea that life could bring monstrous blows, and that these might make a girl question God. We had Exhibit A in our midst, and, if anything, we needed escape from the evidence for a while. Meg needed escape more than anyone else. As the oldest daughter, she was called on more than ever to help out around the house. She had duties and cares. But maybe, when she grew up, all kinds of things would be better. Maybe, like Ethel T. Wead, she would marry a doctor and feel secure. Maybe there would be a cure for MS.

The laughing and hooting, the dirty-old-man act, our general clowning around and obnoxiousness in the bethel had to do with the foreignness of our bodies, these strange new temples. What were we going to do with these female bodies? We looked at fashion magazines and advertisements. We were hungry for hope and laid low by the revelation of our inadequacies. What were boys, men, going to make of us?

Changing into our white robes and back again, skating on the edge of hysteria, we rehearsed for the moment when men would see. All the joking and kidding around were shields for our intense modesty and newfound homelessness within our own bodies. In the dimness of the back room, I caught glimpses of breasts, underpants, thighs, and pretended not to see. This girl was fatter; this girl thin. How was I? In the mirror I saw someone average, mousy really, with plain features and light brown hair.

Despite my high regard for Roy Rogers and the chaste gentlemanliness signified by his being in the world, everything I now heard about boys suggested that every single one of them badly wanted to have sex. But if a girl obliged, no one would ever respect her again, least of all herself. Worse, she could end up pregnant, and that would merely be the end of her life. Couldn't boys just like you and want to be with you constantly? This was what I was willing to offer. But as for the rest, I did not even like kissing. Furthermore, I got out of the slow-dance business soon after satisfying myself that I knew what it was like and that at least one boy would choose me.

I had a new best friend, Andrea. We baked cookies, joined the debate team, sewed ourselves some good wool pants. She rose through the ranks in Job's Daughters—moved through the chairs, it was called—to become the honored queen, the top spot in the bethel organization. She had a crown and a long purple cape to wear over her white robe (white and purple were the Job's colors, as if we were an athletic team).

At the last meeting before we graduated from high school, Andrea relinquished her crown. Someone sang "Sunrise, Sunset" and made us all teary; then there was punch and a white sheet cake. Each piece of cake had a single flower in purple frosting on it.

When we got back into our regular clothes and turned off all the lights, descended the long staircase to leave the bethel for the last time, Andrea and I were emphatically virgins. I think it was exactly the thing Mrs. Mick wanted above everything else, despite all the words we memorized about Job and the Adversary, despite all the songs and the marching around in our regulation robes. We had made the city aud shudder with the electric sounds of delayed gratification. Mrs. Mead would have to agree that we could have done worse.

OZ

IF WE had done it right, the official photograph of me leaving home would have been black and white. But it is mainly pink. I am in the Minneapolis airport about to leave for my freshman year at college. I have on bell-bottomed jeans and a shirt of miniature pink-and-white checks. I am seated beside the cherry-pink Samsonite luggage set I got as a graduation gift. My hair is long. My eyes are pink from tears I am trying to hold back. I love home—our house, the town where I know everyone; the quiet farmland and far horizon, our superb skies rolling with the silent chant of one God, *I am that I am.*

My parents have driven me to this spot in the airport, five hours from our town, but will not get on the plane with me to the East Coast. They cannot leave the paper for this. They cannot spend hundreds of dollars on a flight just to glance around my dorm room and say it is nice and wish me a fun time.

I have done well. I have opportunity. My heart is hollowed out.

. . .

An Emerald City devised with me in mind would have greatly resembled Princeton. The campus was deficient in prairie. Also, it lacked pastures full of palominos. But otherwise the thing had been achieved. The trees, varied, ancient, and profuse, seemed straight from a storybook illustration of the enchanted forest. Unlike the plain elms at home, most had trunks far too thick for one person's arms to encircle. Some were even labeled. They had been transported to the campus with great difficulty thanks, I gathered, to some wealthy alumnus or visiting foreign dignitary—a grateful Chinese person, maybe. I had never seen such trees. I wandered about in a tree stupor.

The dormitories, arranged around stately courtyards that unfolded from one to another, were made mostly of gray stone and festooned with carvings. Many were connected by archways that regularly echoed with singing. Here were all the nooks and crannies I had longed for in my range fantasies of canyons and arroyos. Sometimes the brassy autumn light painted bands of copper and violet across the buildings. But other days were ash-colored with muffled light. The trees looked as though they had been charcoaled into the scene. In the rain, it all smelled like fresh heaven.

It was quickly clear to me that more money than I had ever heard of had been poured into this place. And to my wonderment, it was all devoted to intellectual striving. Princeton was an earthly paradise for smart kids, perhaps in my case the very reward for the faithful alluded to in Job's Daughters. During high school I had researched pollution control and the jury system and unilateral military intervention at night while other kids watched TV. On weekends I had competed in debate tournaments while my classmates screamed their lungs out at the basketball game. While they trolled the gravel roads scouting for good places to kiss or hold keg parties, I spoke extemporaneously on prison reform, inflation, and "Middle East: powder keg."

Now, it seemed, in return for all work and no play, my prize was this Gothic amusement park that had once been home to Albert Einstein. Strolling through the place on those sultry first days, I felt gratitude, even self-congratulation. But feeling at home was another matter.

First came my wrong-footed landing. After much confusion, an irritated airport limousine driver dropped me off. We had already deposited a number of other students near the campus, then driven away, neither of us understanding where I was to go. As we headed down the commercial strip of Route 1, I felt sure this must be wrong, but we kept looking for a place the driver thought was correct—apparently a hotel. When at last he turned around, his snarling unkindness was at least as unsettling to me as the fact of my having drifted off course. At home, people would not dream of handling a stranger roughly, least of all a young girl who was lost. Why did people out here act like this? I rode the rest of the way enfolded in fear. When we got back in town and found the converted hotel that was my freshman dorm, the driver demanded extra money. I gave him nearly all my cash. I found my room and met my roommate while still quaking.

As the days passed, my fear subsided into a low-grade anxiety that over the years has lessened but never entirely left me. Now, I only notice it when I go home: I see the land rearranging itself around me, relaxing into prairie; the sky unfurling back to its proper immensity, like a fresh white sheet snapped over a bed by competent, vigorous arms. The fear drains out of me. I note, with some surprise, that I have been feeling tense.

. . .

Charlie preceded me east. In a development Dickens might have dreamed up, my brother had won a four-year scholarship to Lawrenceville, an elite prep school in New Jersey. His benefactor was the *Minneapolis Tribune,* which he had served as a paperboy in the days when only boys were hired. At that time the *Tribune* sponsored a scholarship competition in much the way it offered free trips to Minnesota Twins games, as an incentive for selling more subscriptions. Charlie liked winning things. He liked seeing how well he could do. And so he signed up to take the test. At fourteen he left the prairie.

"Reginald Carnaby von Thalen, the Third," he said, calling home, telling the name of a friend. Keith, his best friend, was the son of an airline executive. The boys at Lawrenceville had the run of a bucolic campus, a patchwork of emerald playing fields accented by water and wooded areas. The field house, a modern sports temple, featured I don't know how many basketball courts; at home, like nearly all South Dakota towns, we had only one. But what amazed our family most was the swimming pool, an immense, multi-laned affair, bigger than any hotel pool we had seen. We knew of no high school in our entire state that even had a pool.

At Lawrenceville they were dead serious not just about swimming but about every form of physical competition. They had sports we did not know about: squash, rugby, fencing, rowing. One summer Charlie brought home a lacrosse stick, showed how it was held, and started bouncing balls off our house. When he went back in the fall, he had to study hard: They threw "The Red Pony" at him, along with French and advanced calculus.

All the vast and expensive apparatus of Lawrenceville was bent toward one purpose—getting your son into the best possible college on earth. Soon Charlie was advising me on the subject.

He explained about the Ivy League. The main thing, he said, was to get in. The school would help with the money.

The financial-aid application our parents submitted on my behalf revealed relatively little in the income column, despite all their years of both working all day and then going back to the print shop most nights. They were there again on weekends, most of Saturday, part of Sunday. No matter how they slaved, it did not add up to Princeton. And so I was informed by letter that I would have a "work-study" job in the dining hall. It sounded outside my line. Unlike Meg and so many of the girls I grew up with, I never yearned to be a carhop at the drive-in. So I had zero experience in the food-service industry. But if I had to do this dining hall job, I would. What choice did I have? As Charlie had made clear, it was necessary to go to the best possible place.

Alongside the other scholarship kids at what was simply called Commons, I scrubbed silverware in huge plastic tubs, stacked trays on a conveyer belt for washing, brought dirty dishes into the kitchen on carts. Before arriving, I had bought some platform shoes in Minneapolis. I soon saw that they were all wrong fashion-wise. But they were excellent for skating across the slop on the kitchen floor, lifting me a good three inches above the muck.

The kitchen was immense, choking with food smells and steam. In midwinter, we cracked the windows open and drank in the cold air as though it were water. The cooks, mainly men, many of them black, all worked with the same slow, deliberate rhythm, as lost to themselves as the rowers I had seen stroking across Lake Carnegie but wasting even less motion. By the end of the night their white aprons were filthy and their faces moist. When the last diners had been served, they sat down somewhere, anywhere. They had a cigarette or merely regarded the students still on cleanup with heroic irony. We would escape, they knew, but theirs was a lifetime harnessed to macaroni and cake flour bought in bulk, everything stacked by the forkload-full downstairs in receiving.

The cooks' gaze distressed me. In my mind I tried to answer it. First, at least in my own case, escape from hard toil seemed no sure thing. But second, the cooks could not know the extent of my labors to get here. Anyone could work hard. Might not the cooks simply have worked harder in school when they were young? Yet something told me my answers were green ones, the same kind I had come up with for Watts, the answers of a ten-year-old who did not know the world.

Perhaps because it gave me less to ponder, the job I liked best was serving—scooping a starch and mystery meat onto a plate, handing it with a smile to the diner, who was, I had absolute faith, someone special. I plated up chicken fricasee, turkey tetrazinni, and seafood Newburg; I dealt out overcooked broccoli and succotash, hoagy sandwiches with chips, scrambled eggs and sausage.

"Plenty of everything, please," one boy said with a smile every day at lunch. He was tall and skinny, with short hair. I loaded his plate, grateful for his awkward mercy in seeming to want my substandard goods. So many others barely looked at me.

For many weeks, I had trouble finding my way back to my room after my dinner shifts were over. Every sidewalk and footpath, every road, seemed to follow a hidden inclination. The sloping land and the thickness of buildings and trees made it hard to grasp the place whole. The dark made it particularly hopeless.

At home we lived Euclidian-style, as though on graph paper. I could stand on practically any one of our straight streets and see to the edge of town, to the sky pulled down like a shade. At any point in space I could see where I was in relation to the country-side and the horizon. But Princeton kept hiding the vanishing point. My location was only what I saw immediately around me.

One night, after a shift at the graduate college dining room, I became seriously lost. The grad school, marked by a single Gothic tower, stood apart from the campus on a hill. A layer of stately houses and a golf course separated the two. I had been on my feet for several hours and was thankful to be heading for my room. Occasionally in the dark streets, I glimpsed my destination, Princeton Inn. It was far downhill, glowing like a white cruise ship beyond the golf course. There, I would think, getting closer. But then the streets seemed to take me farther away.

The longer I wandered, the more I feared some kind of attack. Maybe robbers and rapists coursed these streets. I tried one route, then another, passing grand houses and houses that were grander still. I wondered what kind of people lived in them—how hard you had to work and at what to achieve such a life. But mostly I only wanted to see something familiar. My heart pumped and finally tears came to my eyes. At length, exhausted, I caught sight of the golf course once more. It was private property not con-nected to the university, and we had been warned not to go on it. But I saw it was the only way. In the darkness, I headed down its long tree-dotted slope toward the only home I had now—the dorm room with the blue clock and red hotpot received as grad-uation gifts, the place with my roommate's map of Scotland on the wall.

When at last I reached the back side of the inn, I was met by a high chain-link fence. I gazed at the inn's brick terrace, could see and hear the students in the common rooms just beyond. I did not want to be seen: lost freshman, crybaby. I looked, I knew, exactly like what I was.

Warm with shame, I made my way along the fence. It went on and on. Clearly, the golfers did not want students gamboling on their high-priced playground. At last came an opening. I hairpinned back, came in through the front door. A walk that should have lasted ten minutes had taken an hour.

I climbed onto my bunk bed and wrapped myself in my green army blanket. I wanted to go home to our house. But already home was swallowed up behind me. Red Sea waters spliced themselves over Sixth Street in the Cecil B. DeMille production that had become my life.

In the morning I went to the terrace and stared in prim daylight across the golf course. The spires of the grad college appeared humiliatingly close. I tried to see what it was, exactly, that had so defeated me; where, in the darkness, I had gone wrong. But it was impossible to tell. Somewhere out there were the leafy lanes where I had circled in confusion. To people I could not imagine, the houses I had passed signified life's greatest reassurance: home. I felt numb with envy. The air was cool and moist, redolent of fall. I tried to pull in extra air, fall air, the only familiar thing.

It was not paradise. We had to work hard, harder than seemed possible. Here was all knowledge, the library seemed to say, help yourself. Figure out how the world works. Figure out how it all fits together. Show us what a genius you are. The library made our sweet little Carnegie confection back home look like a Christmas tree ornament. It was officially called the Harvey E. Firestone Library, and it rose three stories high and also burrowed three floors deep into the earth near Nassau Street.

In purpose and form, the Harvey E. Firestone Library was as far from the Firestone store in my town as it could possibly be. Yet it was fundamentally dependent on that humble establishment and on thousands like it. By weird coincidence, the wellspring of pleasurable memory would now confer pleasures of another kind.

Late in the afternoon I often sat in the reading room watching the other students quietly turn a page or write in a notebook. I sat and thought of how I was behind, also out of place. Some of the girls wore Icelandic wool sweaters in soft blue or pink or emerald green, with yokes knit in a design like snowflakes. They were expensive sweaters, available at a shop on Nassau Street, but I could never get up the nerve to buy one. They were a signal that you came from a certain life and expected certain things.

I knew other financial-aid students who felt the same about Top-Siders, the brown leather moccasins with rubber soles that were so common there seemed to be a free public supply somewhere, like the white-shoe box in the bethel. Top-Siders signaled that your family had a boat. Actually, our family did have one, if you counted the cranky power craft webbed with dead flies that Grandma Tait kept at her lake cottage in Minnesota. We had an aluminum fishing boat also. But topsiders signified a yacht with shiny varnished surfaces, sails the size of clouds, and amenities in the hold. If you could not deliver these things, topsiders were at best a costume and at worst a form of fraud.

Although dress was tricky, it was nothing compared with our task of learning. Two branches of study were offered. The more reliable was thoroughly mapped and promised measurable proficiency: We might master foreign languages or concepts in math and the sciences. The other branch, alarmingly inexact, was deep forest, the essence of what was approvingly called a liberal education. We were to learn to think critically, with reference to history, literature, art, philosophy, and religion. Ultimately, it was this side of knowledge that supplanted the range of my childhood imaginings and drew me with a buzz of expectation to the library.

The main trail in had been blazed by Matthew Arnold, the English poet and critic. In the nineteenth century, he advised that the job of the literary critic was to "propagate the best that is known and thought in the world." At Princeton the idea had been enlarged upon so that "the best that is known and thought" became the liberal arts ideal and the theme of our existence. Some of the younger scholars were chipping away at Arnold's premise. But in my time there, it remained largely undisturbed. It was as though we took all our meals alongside great men, arguing over Plato, Nietzsche, and Freud as if they still lived and might be run into on Cannon Green.

The very first week I was notified that writers were extraordinary beings—people who felt and understood in ways vitally important to everyone else. Without the great writers, we were mere machines who worked, ate, and slept. Certainly I had sampled many of these writers during high school. But it appeared I had not fully seen or been shown their genius. Everything had to do with looking closely, with patient meditation and diving beneath the surface.

Much of the code had been unlocked by literary criticism, a field I had not heard of before arriving at the university. The library was jammed with works of criticism. The professors warned us off. Don't peek, they advised. Form your own ideas on *Crime and Punishment*. They sent us forth to write and interpret, interpret and write, and I did not cheat, look for ideas wiser and subtler than my own, before writing a paper. But oh afterward! I loved criticism. I loved its fine reasoning, its striving after complex truths, and especially its unquestioning belief in the worthiness of the writer's labor. Criticism sent me back to the works themselves with greater wonder and admiration than I had had before.

Within months my plain world, in which only God was great, had been transformed. Before, my mental universe had been trinitarian: one fatherly god, a son who died for our sins, and a holy spirit that moved among us bringing delight and consolation. From this all blessings—and all interpretations—flowed. But by the time the first semester at college ended, it was as though new territory had been opened for settlement alongside the old. Here the great poets, painters, and philosophers pitched tents in a New World colony I was learning to cherish.

Names I had never heard before—Joyce, Mann, Stevens—suddenly rolled like thunder. Phrases of the poets dropped from Princeton's elusive skies or bubbled from the stone lips of gargoyles as I walked to class. *Bee-loud glade* and *morning's minion* and *bird thou never wert. The only emperor is the emperor of ice cream.* I got to the lecture hall early, saw only a fragment of daylight through the leaded-glass windows, and waited to be lost in waters gloriously over my head.

At the heart of my discovery lay a paradox. Keats, with his doctrine of negative capability, had left it marked on the trail. To create, an artist had to commit an act of self-erasure. But then, it seemed, upon resurfacing, he (and it was never she) became a great man, a kind of super-self. At one level I easily grasped the idea. It seemed a restatement of the Christian message, which is that selflessness yields the greatest riches. But what rewards exactly were to come to an artist? They could not be only spiritual;

otherwise, as a practical matter, no art could be made. An artist had to earn money.

Most of the time, I set this question aside. I wanted to be a pure believer. But I was troubled by the cooks' gaze and by many things I could not see. Just what sacrifices of spirit and character had to be made to earn a living? I feared, much of the time, that they must be immense. But at other times I suspected I was religion's fool. A small income was no more a sign of goodness than was showing up for church each week. So why not find a job that paid well? Every spring the corporations came to pluck the seniors from the tree, starting them off at good salaries. Why not be one of these?

And yet, wouldn't more be expected of a person with a good job—longer hours, a Disneyland smile? And suppose that person had only poetry or painting in mind all day long. Would she not be cheating the company? Far from offering solutions on how to live, Princeton proposed that it was a bigger problem than I had imagined.

If art and religion were conflated, it was partly the fault of the architecture. The campus had an air of perpetual Sunday. The doorways resembled church entrances; the cloister walks evoked monastic life. The chapel, more truly a cathedral, occupied a central spot just opposite the library and nearly within the embrace of the English department. Inside it for the first time I looked up and up at arches revealing the unexpected delicacy of stone. The profusion of stained glass figures ratified my growing suspicion that there was too much to know. Simply too much had happened. The symbols of Western civilization were so numerous that they ran together and became the jeweled mush of a broken kaleidoscope. If you needed a reminder of the wasteland feeling, the chapel was the place to go.

Sometimes I did go, but mainly for the quiet. The chapel seemed breathless, as though listening for chord changes in the music of the spheres. Noble light filtered in. One day I noticed my belief was escaping, floating up like a red balloon to the chapel ceiling. God remained, with magnified mystery and a greater capacity to inspire fear. But the Christian system of thought was now open, like all others, to critical inquiry. I felt cold and bereft. God the loving father, on whose care we might lean and who provided a place for us in heaven, was not assured. He became, instead, unknowable—an actor dimly felt, a ceaseless question—a presence, more often absence, I appealed to without end. My hometown had equipped me with Christ, a portable tent I had somehow mislaid. With that gone, it felt as if nearly everything was directly between me and God. And God, I was learning, had a side.

No writer wrestled harder with God than Tolstoy. But that was not the first thing I found out about him. The first was *Anna Karenina*—first through eighth, in fact; all eight sections and 740 pages of the Aylmer Maude translation. It was the fall of my sophomore year, and everything gave way to this single reading experience. *Anna Karenina* was a complete world, down to food and dress, thought and impulse. Everything, it seemed, was included. Tolstoy had gotten his arms around not just any tree but some ancient lord of the forest. He could shake his own hand if he chose.

Anna Karenina was more than a mere catalogue of the world's contents. Its creator had whittled at the human psyche, freeing the tailings before our eyes. And it was not Anna or Karenin or Vronsky, or any of the many others in the book that we beheld, finally, in their essence. Rather it was the panorama of our own selves, with their vast uncharted zones. If the mind were a house, it would be fair to say that there was not one room Tolstoy had failed to visit. And not only did he visit; he took precise note of how the pictures were arranged, of the stain on the carpet and the mismatched chairs. I read *Anna Karenina* with amazement, with such annoyance at any distractions that I might have been sprawled in front of a *Fury* episode. I read slowly and with difficulty, aged in the process; I struggled with the historical context and the reports from realms of experience not yet mine. I felt belittled by the book's magnitude, at the same time enlarged: a human being had made this, had created a world stuffed with life and clanging with incongruous hope. The central fact of the story, a suicide, was completely overcome by the sheer achievement of Tolstoy's art. This was what it was possible to do with writing, I realized when I came to the end. This was the Pacific at last.

It is the job of students to find idols and passionately defend them. "Not as good as Tolstoy," I would say after that Russian autumn when I was nineteen, as though each new book I read had been written with no other purpose than to depose the king of my personal mountain. I took his case to the handful of students I knew who, like me, were besotted with literature. We read and compared, urged new works on one another. I looked for something ultimate, some great unifying theme to serve as a guide through life. Others wanted only a new experience, new possibilities. I did not see how they could stand to leave things banging, like unlocked gates.

We knew who everybody was, the ones who wanted to write. Most, because it seemed so presumptuous, were careful not to speak of it. A few thought writing could be a club thing, the Round Table at the Algonquin. They joined the Nassau Lit. The rest of us generally steered clear of one another, would have preferred whole continents between. Seeing one another reminded us too painfully of our outlandish hopes, of our unsteady voices that cracked and broke when we tried, alone, to practice.

Yet who was to say that one of us would not succeed, would not become another Tolstoy? After all, there was a time in Tolstoy's life when he was young—unruly, passionate, drifting. Tolstoy was not yet Tolstoy. Where was the evidence, so far, that it could not happen for one of us?

Unfortunately, my hero's life contained numerous disturbing facts. It was not like mine in key ways. And I had to admit that Tolstoy did not seem like a very nice guy. Both of his parents died when he was still a child. As a young man, he sampled war, going to the Caucasus to play soldier. He was a carouser who contracted venereal disease before you could say Jack Spratt, a spendthrift who left too much of the family fortune at the gaming table, a screw-up who could not buckle down to his studies or choose a career path.

He lectured the women he considered for marriage as if they were auditioning for a show. And when he finally selected Sofya Bers, he preferred, on the whole, her sprightly younger sister. Once Sofya had accepted his proposal, he rushed her into marriage. First, though, he gave her his diaries to read. They chronicled all his exploits with other women and made her cry. The day of the wedding, he arrived at the Bers apartment saying he had doubts, that they could still call the marriage off. He delayed his appearance that evening at the church. Sofya Bers cried through the service and cried when they got into the coach that would take them to Yasnaya Polyana, the Tolstoy family estate. She was eighteen.

Before it was over, they would have figured out a thousand different ways to torture each other. And she would be sixty-five.

Tolstoy was deeply divided. On one side was his stupendous appetite for life; on the other, profound guilt and a drive to renounce the world, thereby winning God's grace. The divided part was what I understood, or thought I did. I had a double soul, in constant war with itself. Spiritual or secular? Midwest or Northeast? A life of comfort or the life of the mind? The meaning of Tolstoy was that you could spin off all the contradictory pieces of yourself and form them into a whole through fiction. You would not have to choose, only contain.

In his own life, however (and for me this was more unwanted news), Tolstoy began to choose. As he proceeded through middle age, he renounced his great works, including *Anna Karenina,* as immoral productions. This confused and troubled me. I had just come from the God-swathed land he was setting out for. We were passing each other on the way, might have waved hello from the windows of our train cars.

As Tolstoy became more of a Tolstoyan, the gulf between him and Countess Sofya widened. He wanted to transfer Yasnaya Polyana to her so that he would at last truly have nothing. On June 18, 1884, Sofya asked him why he had so many horses. If one was so lowly, why all these horses?

As my dad would say, that tore it. Tolstoy left, meaning never to come back. He had left before, but this time it was for good, he assured everyone. He did come back though; Sofya was pregnant with their twelfth child. The baby turned out to be a girl, Alexandra. By the time she died, I had been out of college for two years, and my mind was thronged with so many writers I could not figure out a thing. What a noise they made, what a drumming of hooves as they roared across the plain.

Here is how I would put things now.

SIMILARITIES BETWEEN ME AND TOLSTOY:

- Divided soul.
- Dogged by the God question.
- Dream of encompassing an entire world in writing.
- Disgust, verging on mortification, at own writing. Here is a typical note Tolstoy jotted down about his creations on June 14 (my eventual birthday) in the year 1894: "Read through all the works of fiction which I've begun. They're all bad."

DIFFERENCES BETWEEN ME AND TOLSTOY:

- Large beard (him).
- Large family fortune (him).
- Results.

That first spring Princeton pelted us with beauty. Forsythia and rhododendron, dogwood, magnolia, weeping cherry trees—all of it was new to me and nameless. Youth compounded the damage. Our senses were fresh and available for ravishing as they never would be again. I was in love, helpless to focus. As in some medieval system devoted to chastity, our restraints tightened: The academic demands piled higher. In the same cloud of unspecified yearning as everyone else, I labored on, sitting up late to type papers, imprisoning myself in the library while the sun lay siege through the windows.

I fell for a senior boy I knew I could not keep. He was handsome and dangerous, with a red sports car. There were dramatic scenes overlaid by my reading of D. H. Lawrence. And yet, even as I was swept up in all this heightened feeling, I sensed a falseness not far from the surface. Scholarship proposed that romantic love was a creation of the troubadors—essentially a passing fiction. When, in the nineteenth century, religious belief became seriously lost to the world, romantic love was left as the consolation prize. Everyone wanted not God but the big sunlit-valley sensation of being in love.

Yet how could such Olympian dramas play out? I thought of the adults in my hometown, their marriages, and could recall no signs of grand passion. Instead, I saw tidy bundles of duty and habit, bound up by the censoring eyes of neighbors. Marital love existed, I felt sure, but it was a lamp turned low. Anything that strayed beyond was too risky and too silly for the farm towns of the Midwest.

But what about this new place? The people seemed genuinely and plausibly different—they were cultured and complex. Perhaps they were the kind among whom all-consuming and tragic love could take root. I did read *Madame Bovary,* for class; I even understood how we were to take it. *Madame Bovary* was the supreme indictment of bourgeois life and the romantic illusions that can fester there. I just did not like the idea. I did not want it—in those days of flowering trees and poetry and finally having a boyfriend—to mean me.

We lived in layers of historical time. The buildings evoked the Middle Ages. The windows opened on iron hinges and lacked screens. The first whiff of winter thaw set you on the road to Canterbury. Air liquored with magnolia came inside, along with the smell of cut grass and sometimes bees.

But there was, too, a Jazz Age overlay that settled in occasionally like a sudden change in the weather. We girls were still new to the campus. On some weekends, and continuing a tradition that preceded us, buses full of well-bred young ladies from all-female schools would arrive, as if to remind us that the whole point was and ever would be getting a husband. "Imports" we called them; we glowered and made fun, refused to doll ourselves up.

At such times, the reigning spirit belonged to F. Scott Fitzgerald. In Fitzgerald's day Princeton was almost exclusively a place for rich boys. A half-century later their ghostly presence still pervaded the place, as though they were its true possessors, its unshakable essence. That essence was aristocratic, romantic, and male. Girls were permitted only for fun, and they had better be pretty.

Fitzgerald himself was beautiful, with a patrician profile that has been captured in a famous photograph. He was also an instant success, with a first novel published to great acclaim when he was still in his early twenties. *This Side of Paradise* was quoted liberally during alumni events and in official publications. It was the document meant to form our deepest conceptions about Princeton: We were to love it unreservedly and preferably by moonlight.

Somewhere in my admissions packet it was suggested that I might want to read *This Side of Paradise* before I arrived. I dutifully did so and could feel the tug of another transformation. Just as, for maximum happiness, range life required me to be Roy Rogers, it appeared that college life needed me to be a beautiful and well-to-do young man.

By writing about the place, Princeton's most famous dropout had managed to claim it. I rejected Fitzgerald's idea that he was an outsider by virtue of being from the Midwest. To me, a rich Midwesterner was a contradiction in terms. The same went for an urban Midwesterner, which Fitzgerald was. St. Paul, Minnesota, had its own version of a privileged class, with its own set of private addresses. And these places were as unreachable from Plainville as any villa in Spain.

To me Fitzgerald was a full-fledged insider, the insider who imagined being an outsider—Jay Gatsby—just for fun. More outside than that—female, for example—he did not dream of bothering with.

It was new for Princeton to admit young women. But it was also relatively new for it to admit blacks, Asians, Hispanics, and Jews, or anyone not from a world of privilege. SAT scores did not entirely supplant a wealthy background. But they were starting to supplement it. Princeton was taking more students from public schools, and certain confusions were beginning to form.

Nevertheless, and partly thanks to Fitzgerald's eager mythologizing, the old social hierarchy stood firm. Social rankings were as fixed as in Shakespeare. WASP was higher than Catholic (alas, poor Scott) and higher than Jew; private school trumped public; white was better than black; old money was better than new. East Coast was better than West. And male was better than female. (With few exceptions, the minds we studied and praised were male.)

Not a few of us questioned it, turning our course work into the very weapon that would chip away at these distinctions. Still, the oldest assertion against social rank stood close to hand. Christianity—which Tolstoy correctly saw as the most radically democratic of institutions—was symbolized at Princeton by the spectacular structure so modestly called the chapel. But the chapel's sheer grandeur implied that the message it was built to proclaim either required some revision or should not be taken entirely seriously.

Belief might vanquish architecture. But mine had floated off.

In its absence, I earnestly embraced what seemed the university's chief value: We were to pursue the life of the mind. Yet every day was a struggle to assert this priority against the social order. I would leave class thinking of Montaigne, revolving the importance of the name, only to hear some fair-haired princess pronounce the equally important name of Hampton.

Who were the Hamptons? Why were people always going to see them? In the spring of my freshman year, I heard that Lionel Hampton was going to play at the graduation dance by the Wilson School fountain. But he sounded unrelated.

Eventually, I was instructed that the Hamptons corresponded to Fitzgerald's West and East Egg in *The Great Gatsby*. Wealth had its own geography and an entire field of references that became part of my education whether I wished it or not. People spoke of Aspen, Provence, and Zermatt, Paris and London, Nantucket and the Vineyard. Winnetka, Westchester, Darien.

"Where in North Dakota are you from again?"

I would state the name of my town, amid polite nods. I knew, by their eyes, which ones were dealing me out.

No matter how all-encompassing the monastic raptures of late-night learning, by morning the ordained social order had settled anew over the life of the university. It was as immobile as the handsome stone buildings, and you could not overcome it by knowing your Milton better than the Vitabath heiress down the hall knew hers.

The eating clubs were the ultimate expression of this other life we lived—the life that sorted and evaluated us after we had studied and figured and written until our eyes burned, turned in our papers, and been judged in that way. Through the process called Bicker, sophomores vied to be accepted into one of these clubs—to get a "bid" after a week of meeting and greeting. (One club accepted anyone who wished to join—a new development considered radical and immediately looked down upon.) The alternative, for people who could not submit or afford the few extra thousand dollars it cost to join a club, was to "go independent" starting in their junior year. This meant perhaps purchasing a meal plan at Commons, where the underclassmen ate; sharing one of the new suites that featured kitchens; or doing a combination of things—snacking in one's room or catching meals on the fly at the student center or in restaurants.

I went independent. I lived on the same floor as a senior who stopped by my room one day in early fall to get acquainted. He was from a nearby town in Pennsylvania, where he had gone to a public high school. His surname was Italian—for all I knew he was descended from one of the stone masons who had been brought from overseas to erect, with exquisite craft, these buildings in which we now lived.

Just above his mouth was a large mole, which was what I focused on as the senior boy talked, because after a while your eyes had to go somewhere. I did not know Pennsylvania towns and could not picture the Mole's place. When he spoke of his school's excellent lab facilities, all I could see were the ones in Mr. Nelson's school in Minnesota.

The Mole wore Top-Siders. He spoke warmly about his eating club. He said that what he especially enjoyed about the club was being served by black waiters (a longstanding tradition still in effect at some of the more selective ones).

I groped for a reply.

"I know," he said, grinning, a gleam of mock apology in his eye. "But I really like it." He spied the expensive grocery store fruit I had purchased as a treat and arranged in a basket on top of my trunk. "Mind if I grab an apple?" he said.

I let him. He made me sick.

I never knew when the Mole's thundering stereo would erupt. But noise had always bothered me. In fact, it was my need for quiet, and especially for solitude, that had led me away that year from two kind roommates to a single room. For juniors the academic demands increased: We were obliged to do independent work while continuing with our regular course loads. My choices, when the Mole's noise began, were to (1) pound on his door and then, when he opened it, politely request quiet, or (2) flee to the library, avoiding confrontation. I dreaded speaking up; usually I fled.

One spring day I found myself pounding on the Mole's door without result. The noise was shattering: It filled the halls and rattled the doors and windows. I had just settled in to work; now I had no choice but to collect my things and head for the library. Outdoors, I was stunned to see the Mole lying shirtless in sunglasses in the courtyard that my room overlooked. His room faced the opposite way, onto the street. For him to hear his music in the courtyard, the volume had to be turned as high as it would go.

What could be said?

My moral training, my unassertive Midwestern upbringing, was no good. *Be nice. Be kind. Forgive.* I was like a scrap of paper. For months it had gone on like this. I had no regular place to eat, and my room was at best a provisional haven. More and more, it resembled some box at the psych lab designed for operant conditioning experiments. I would, from time to time, receive a shock (the Mole's loud music). Only unlike in operant conditioning, and try as I might to predict, I never knew when the shock was coming. For much of the year, I drifted about the campus with my hopeless workload in my arms, looking for places where I could get it done.

When I got home that summer, I was afraid to leave the house. In the fall the Mole was gone, off to medical school. I moved to the only all-girls dorm on campus and gained a measure of peace. But by then I was emptied out. By then it seemed to me that I was always trembling inside. I could not have said why. And I could not imagine how I would finish the year.

On football weekends, families came. Many students had fathers, grandfathers, uncles, brothers, cousins, who had gone to Princeton. They lived close enough to drive to town for the game. They brought fine picnics of rare roast beef sandwiches lightly dressed with horseradish; they brought smoked salmon and wheels of Brie. Some could not do without crystal, linen napkins, silver champagne buckets. They dressed in beautiful wool plaids and tweeds. The mothers had expensive jewelry and pretty scarves expertly knotted. "Tailored," Meg would have said, confidently pigeonholing the look. The fathers brought sheltering experience and advice.

I seldom went to the game, but wherever I was studying that day, the distant roar from the stadium, the sound of drums and brass, made my heart strangely ache. The closing scenes of *Jude the Obscure* worked an identical effect on me late one afternoon as I read in a library window niche and, as a result, missed dinner. I know of no good name for this longing to be with the crowd and a part of things. But if you come from a small Midwestern town, it never leaves you. And if you endure four years at Princeton, it gets repackaged in tiger-striped paper. Here is the fearful symmetry that William Blake wrote about, a symmetry of connection and estrangement, love and hate.

A spirit can empty out, but it can also fill up again, as mine did by the end of that final senior year. Today, mostly, we speak of such things clinically. Anyone thumbing through the Diagnostic and Statistical Manual of the American Psychiatric Association might have come up with a label for my troubles. I only know that to hold itself together, my mind worked through a heavy symbolizing period, in which nothing seemed random or coincidental. I encountered every lion, tiger, and bear with due terror. But the Emerald City, when I did catch sight of it, was gorgeous and satisfying indeed, at once within me and external. To a mystic, all worldly concerns fall away, yielding to what cannot ever truly be described, although many have tried. I would notate it only as an excess of meaning. I felt it, told no one, wondered if I was crazy. Not long afterward, I had my diploma.

Did Oz belong to Dorothy, who traveled there out of psychic need? Or did it belong to those who had always lived there—the Munchkins and their queen, the wizard who, it was said, could grant anybody's most profound wish?

How do we properly claim a place—and why do we so long to make a place ours? Why are we appalled when someone not like us wishes to claim the same place?

Whose Princeton was it?

One warm night, after an evening across Nassau Street at the Annex, a popular bar, I walked back to the campus quite late with a small group of friends. It was the end of my sophomore year, the year of Tolstoy. I had had my first drink, a glass of sherry, and felt pleasantly cheered. With us was Ray, a young Asian-American who was new to me. He was on the verge of graduating and had done brilliantly, I learned in the discreet way such things were almost immediately telegraphed from one Princeton student to another.

Tolstoy, I said.

"Tolstoy!" said Ray, sibilant with exasperation and slapping one hand to his forehead. "My God, he's so didactic!"

Didactic? But how could it be? Was it didactic to show life in a perfect mirror? I started to protest.

Ray was tipsy. "And so we beat on," he suddenly declaimed to the dark skies, to heavy masses of leaves, as we passed through the gate in front of Nassau Hall.

". . . boats against the current. . . ."

Ray had majored in one of the sciences, but now the entire closing of *The Great Gatsby* rolled off his tongue in accented English. Whether Fitzgerald's words were caressed by Chinese or Korean inflections I was too ignorant to know. But this was a voice the Princeton of Fitzgerald would never have expected to hear.

"And so we beat on," Ray began again. We were all laughing uncontrollably, drowning him out. "And so we beat on." He gestured insistently, taking on the great man and putting him away, diminishing Fitzgerald as only the living may do to the dead: *You may have written it just right, captured the place as no one ever will again, but it is we who are young now; we who breathe the incomparable air of this night, this place.*

The massive brick wings of Nassau Hall took form in the gloom. Ray seemed so small as we continued past it beneath the towering trees. Yet how easily our group had walked, with some surprise, through the usually locked front gate. We were gifted test takers or extracurricular phenoms from all over the country, alike only in our frantic drive to do well and to please our parents. To be sure, Princeton had plenty of students who disdained appearing to try too hard. But we were the other kind; for better or worse, a new kind.

Whose Princeton was it?

The fight was hand to hand, minute by minute. I do not have to visit to know that it goes on still. Step off the train, and it is not long before you will see an elderly man, dignified in every way but one. His necktie sports miniature tigers and his umbrella is orange and black. His eyes have the gleam of possession. He will not hear of another Princeton—yours, for instance. The crowd he is determined to be part of is fenced off by memory, a pure, sweet haven in which his values are unquestioned. The sun falls warmly on Blair Arch as he recalls that the train stop once was there. *Then boys: then, it was paradise.*

When it was over, the four years gone, I moved to Cambridge, Massachusetts. I had two trunks containing my Tolstoy and all the other examples of a writer's life; some clothes; a small crystal owl given as a graduation gift by my roommate's mother. I felt flimsy, as though I could be blown away with the slightest breath. I barely cohered.

On a day in early autumn a granddaughter of Niels Ebbesen Hansen helped me pick up my bike, which had been shipped from Princeton to the Boston train station. The granddaughter, Peggy Kilmartin, had come east well before me, to Radcliffe. With her application she had enclosed a polite note requesting the return of her processing fee should Radcliffe be disinclined to admit a girl from Brookings, S.D. Now she was married to a professor at MIT and raising three boys. Just as I thought of Niels Hansen as Grandpa Hansen, I knew Peggy Kilmartin simply as Aunt Peggy.

She was quick and sure, surprisingly strong, as she hoisted my bike into the back of her station wagon. Within seconds we were under way. Aunt Peggy maneuvered with confidence through Boston's harrowing traffic. "At some point," she said, taking in everything about me, "you lose your innocence. And that is that." She said it as though life was possible afterward, that it could even be quite fine.

When we got to Cambridge, the sky was blue and the leaves golden. The sharp air promised clear thinking and an easy time. Aunt Peggy's face filled with joy.

"When I was a student," she said, "it seems to me that every day was like this."

And so it was, exactly so, in the land of Oz.

NORTHEAST CORRIDOR

THE SEVEN o'clock roars through without stopping. The horn is loud in our house, an urban substitute for the rooster's wake-up call. The rush of the train rattles the Limoges Grandma Tait bought at some antique sale or other, then stored in the cabinet under her TV. We were quite surprised to find it after she died.

The seven o'clock is the night owl train from Washington to Boston. The passengers, stiff and sleepy, must begin to rouse themselves when they pass our house; they have almost reached their destination. After a night on the train, they will be in no mood for arrival. They will wish they were home instead. The exception, always, is any person going to meet a lover. Then there is a fluttering in the stomach, a heightened state of alert. Clacking joy. Hope without circumference.

Better you than me, I think, as I brace for the horn. I have seven rooms and peonies in the yard. I would not want to be on that train again.

. . .

Boston and Washington are the poles of Northeast consciousness. Everything in between has relevance. The rest of the country is vacation spots, hometowns, and dead space. Northeast consciousness is not so much the truth as an artifact of an Eastern education. You must decide where, in the Northeast, you will get a job and live. Leaving the Northeast means your aspirations are not truly serious. The best that can be said is that you are deliberately choosing an alternative lifestyle.

Near the end of college, I found myself aiming toward Boston. There was a house I could share for the summer with people I knew, two women who had already graduated. I had visited the city a few times and found it more manageable (less frightening) than New York. I had no job and no idea of one. I wanted to be a writer, and writing, I knew, was not what most employers wanted done. I guessed I would find some job and try to write at night.

Princeton is a place of grays and deep green. But Boston is red and blue. The red is brick, ubiquitous in buildings and sidewalks. Boston's narrow streets offer glimpses of blue sky, where white seagulls wheel. The subway, where it surfaces to cross the Charles, bisects a dramatic blue vista of river and sky, the river spanned by red bridges, flanked by red buildings. In summer, white boats crowd the water.

From where I was situated in Cambridge, everything seemed an extension of Harvard. (My first job, a secretarial position at the law school, literally was that.) The subway rolled past Mass General Hospital, where the students from Harvard's medical school wound up, and ended downtown, where there were law offices, consulting firms, advertising agencies, and publishing houses.

For a city—that is, a place where I was regularly terrified of losing my life—Boston was oddly cozy. My housemate Nora said the basic rule of thumb was that you could walk anywhere in the city you needed to go, as long as you had the time. Boston and Cambridge, technically two cities, were one to me, Cambridge being the tail that wagged the dog.

The whole place was crowded with effort—the kind I had learned to give at Princeton and believed I must never stop giving. I knew nothing about careers; other than Aunt Peggy, tucked far off in Newton, I knew no adults of whom to ask advice. And in her case, I felt timid. I wandered the streets of the city, wondering what they did in this building or that, trying from the building to figure out the life. Aside from the professions, what were the good jobs and how were they obtained? I answered ads, called up employment agencies. I wrote to the newspapers and Boston's few publishing companies, to the *Atlantic Monthly* magazine. No one had a job for me. The small stake my parents had given me was running out fast, and so I retreated to the familiarity of the university. Harvard had a huge appetite for office help; by midsummer I was back to work-study, only this time it was without the study part, at least formally.

I kept going on my own. I saw myself as a student still, but un-enrolled. I haunted the textbook sections of the Harvard Coop, studying what books were being assigned for courses. I was terri-fied of somehow falling behind. New critical trends in literary studies were forming, and I believed I needed to stay on top of them. I needed to be ready.

That first summer Cambridge fit my notion of the ideal place to live. I had never seen so many bookstores. And they were open at all hours. In cafés that served strong, excellent coffee, you could sit at a tiny table discussing Jung, Marilyn French, or *Moby-Dick* for as long as you pleased. At the next table they were discussing Barthes and Foucault. No one had anything normal to say.

Our Bodies, Ourselves came out. Women went about in Danskin leotard tops, which they wore with jeans or peasant skirts. Some had stopped shaving their legs and underarms. They had a bone to pick with the whole feminine idea.

Lunch was soup and salad, with big slabs of bread you cut from the loaf yourself. Everyone was famished by two-thirty. Going to get ice cream was as big a part of life as going to do laundry.

This unenrolled life on the margins of Harvard, with its books and constant talk of ideas, became my new home. I had been taught well that the life of the mind was the only life worth living, and I meant to be faithful. And yet, on my secretary's salary, nearly everything was denied—not least the books I wanted to buy, and by the armful. (The library was no good: I wanted possession: *Buddenbrooks, I and Thou, The Viking Portable Nietzsche*—they should be there to have and to hold, I believed, from this day forward.)

Though I was thrifty and careful, my weekly paycheck never seemed to stretch far enough. It barely covered my expenses. I thought unavoidably, ashamedly, about money. (Ashamedly, because Thoreau and so many others I had learned to venerate—not to mention Christ of the gravy portrait—had taught that its satisfactions were corrupting and illusory.) As in Princeton, I was surrounded by wealth. Despite the hordes of students living temporarily on a shoestring, plenty were not.

I haunted Harvard Square's fashionable clothing shops for wool skirts and sweaters on sale, checked shoe prices on my lunch hour, rarely bought. Especially, I gazed regularly at the housewares—beautiful glasses from the smallest cordials to the largest water goblets, bright-colored plastic plates, and the stylish out-of-the-question couches accented with crayon-bright Marimekko pillows. It seemed that there was no end to what I could want—could in fact use—yet it was going to take a lifetime to furnish even a modest apartment. In my small studio, I had a rug and my two trunks. The landlord had loaned me a desk and chair, but I seldom wrote; from where I lay on the rug, I could look out the single window that faced Ware Street. I saw a bit of the brick apartment building just across from me, a scrap of blue sky, and occasionally a seagull. There was no ground at all.

My apartment, barely two blocks from the house I had shared over the summer, was all mine and a honey. It was also a miracle. In Cambridge in those days the law of apartments was that they were all taken. By the time you read an ad for one, it was rented. By early summer I had a job, but when September came, no place to live. In my off-duty hours I walked and walked, trying to track down advertised places that, when I got there, seemed either nonexistent or so dangerous that I would need a large fierce dog for protection. My search was fruitless and went on for weeks. One day when my feet seemed unusually achy, I sat down on a patch of grass, took off a shoe, and found that one of them was bleeding. I looked at it, then stared out at the busy street. I was defeated. What was the use of having a job but no place to live?

I would leave. I would go home, to Minneapolis. I felt quite serene about it. I was certain this was failure—I was not fit for the Northeast; my bleeding foot was the proof. But I was not at all prepared for the melting pleasure I felt in failure's embrace. Perhaps the same flood of relief comes with drowning, an extravagant giving in after the last hope has been stilled.

The next day my roommate Marie, who had watched my struggles with quiet dark eyes, announced that she had made inquiries. A studio apartment was opening up just down the block on the top floor of an old brick three-story building. The man to see about it ran the grocery store. I went immediately, scanned the two rooms and bath, and took it on the spot, even though the rent would take half my income each month. As he showed me about, the landlord seemed half apologetic, not at all like a man who was offering deliverance.

Later, I stood alone on the sidewalk, shuddering in the hot sun. I would not retreat after all. I would cling to this new world by my fingernails, in a place of my own. I tried to tell whether this was fate: the close hand of God who, in Ethel T. Wead Mick's version of things, can never resist testing us. It was a call I felt unequipped to make. But on that day I entertained the thought that mercy existed, like some fine trace element we know of from the periodic table, even if we have not seen it with our own eyes.

The apartment had one main room and a small kitchen. I often sat in the kitchen, with its trio of bay windows and the small oak table I bought after several months of making do with my trunk. The table came from an antique shop and was flecked with paint and nailpolish. It was a classic kitchen-table shape, with two leaves folding down on either side.

At this table I fitfully resumed writing. I felt leaden, heavy with the unlikelihood of success. Often, instead of writing, I read pages of an enormous biography of Simone Weill. I scarcely recalled a word from one day to the next. But I was pinned in place by the fear that I was going soft, that the life of the mind I had hoped to sustain was evaporating. There were more years of dull obedience in me than of independent thought. I could so easily revert, the way tall grass reclaimed forsaken prairie homesteads.

The kitchen windows were large, with only shades to cover

them. They offered a fuller view than the window in the next room did of the lives across the way. The street was so narrow I may as well have had my nose flat against the building opposite mine. It was blond brick with a flat roof, ornate window trim, and a topping of sky. I could see a couple taking turns cooking. Cambridge felt like the course catalogue come to life: In every crowded apartment, it seemed to me, people had chosen their specialties and were winging toward expertise. I, meanwhile, sat at my table staring out.

One clear fall day I glanced down to see a young woman strolling slowly by, as though in a trance. Her hair was long. She wore gold hoop earrings, a long down coat belted at the waist, and stylish boots with a heel. She looked perfect. She looked as though she had reached the perfect moment in her life. She gazed about, taking in the street, the stately architecture, perhaps even the turret that topped my apartment like a child's birthday hat. On her face was a look of gratitude.

I knew her.

"Deb!" I wanted to call out. Should I run down the three flights and stop her, say hello? Say "Remember me?"

She was from South Dakota. I had met her during high school debate competitions. I had admired her, joked with her, congratulated her on wins and commiserated over losses. Deb was as bright as she could be, a star of her team. She must have left the state for college, though I never heard where. Perhaps she was here now for the law school; perhaps she had gotten into Harvard Law.

She did not look damaged in any way—in the way I felt—only happy.

I sat motionless in my kitchen chair.

Slowly, hands in her pockets, her face glowing, the young

woman I had known as a girl passed by. She was in Cambridge, Massachusetts, a place of tradition and history, where the streets were narrow, the architecture barnacled with detail; a place where strange languages were heard everywhere and the fragrances of unfamiliar spices wafted from restaurants and apartments. Deb had made it out, had earned this place, by pushing her talents to their utmost. She was a child of the SATs, National Merit Scholarship competitions, American Legion Oratory contests. Now Harvard lay sprawled at her feet. She picked her way through like a princess who has sneaked out in disguise to explore her kingdom.

Utterly torn, I sat completely still. It was as though I feared she might hear me move, as though one peep from me might break the spell. Deb walked on to the corner and disappeared. I never saw her again.

Meg came. She had spent her college years bouncing among Midwestern colleges and emerged with a nursing degree. Now she wanted to try the East. (The East, Midwesterners say, with a combination of reverence and resentment.) Maybe Meg's destiny lay in the East. She had Aunt Peggy to steady her, adult help. Instant roots. Meg loaded her little red car with her things and set out hoping she was leaving all dissatisfactions behind.

I was terrified.

I did not know how I could mix my old life with the new. Maybe the new—the life of the mind, the world of ideas so laboriously entered in what already seemed too short a time—would be borne off in a cloud of Midwestern who-do-you-think-you-are. Or maybe my friends would become Meg's, leaving me in the role of bystander once more. What if Cambridge ceased to be Cambridge and instead became high school, where Meg fit in, attracted boys, and I did not? I knew my feelings were unreasonable. I felt them anyway.

Meg got a job at Mount Auburn Hospital, in Cambridge. She found a tiny studio apartment of her own just off Charles Street on Beacon Hill. She made it cozy with a crocheted afghan she had brought with her and a fabric wall hanging purchased in a trendy design store. She had a little table and two chairs painted black.

Exactly and mysteriously, the bathroom exuded the combination of cleaning and toiletry fragrances I remembered from the Sees' Sixth Street house. It filled my senses, made me shudder with happy displacement. Meg's place was a little Proustian patch of home. Her car, which she increasingly judged impractical, was wedged into a tiny parking space. It had a parking permit sticker. Twice her license plates were stolen—for the novelty we immediately realized, even as we could not get over the shock and meanness of the theft. The plates said South Dakota. They signified a place where bikes were left outside overnight and doors were rarely locked—trust in the goodness of others. Why not just plunder a church while you are at it?

Meg dug in. She developed crushes, went out for drinks with nurse friends, volunteered as an usher so she could see theatrical productions for free. Her favorites were all-dance shows. We met for drinks or shopping or dinner sometimes, compared notes: home vs. here. But she had her own life and so did I.

One night we drank too much wine, staggered to Quincy Market, laughed until we were afraid we might wet our pants. The times with Meg were some of the best ones I ever had. Only our futures, we both sensed, belonged to different worlds. We were like two soldiers from the same hometown assigned to different campaigns. In the end, feeling at home in Boston was even harder for Meg than it was for me. When she gave up, I felt failure threatening me once more. Only this time it was that I had failed my childhood friend.

At the southern terminus of the Northeast Corridor, so named by the train service, lies Washington, the city of white buildings. Every day, strangers settle in, adopting the place as home. No one really belongs, and so everyone does. Some years ago a town official I know in Rhode Island went to Washington to finish his education. He needed a job to pay his expenses. Within a day he was giving guided tours of a city he had never seen.

I went mainly to see my boyfriend. Because Washington has a low landscape and a policy that nothing in its center may be built higher than the Washington Monument, I saw prairie. There were museums in place of cornfields and long government buildings in place of shelter belts. The city's layout, with its avenues radiating like spokes from the Capitol, had more logic to it than Boston's. The main thing, the thing that made me regard Washington as a desirable home, was that you could see great distances. Within the city, from points all along the mall, you could get a view of the horizon. Boston, like Princeton, had none.

The sensation of openness is equally available from the air. A plane circling to land at National Airport provides distinct views of the Washington Monument, the Capitol, the White House, the Lincoln Memorial, and the Jefferson. All are generously spaced apart. "It gets me, every time," Hubert Humphrey once said of this aerial view. I do not think he was talking only about the symbolism. Hubert Humphrey grew up in Dolan, South Dakota, a town even smaller than mine. Open space would have looked right to him and made him feel at home.

Because of my job at the law school, I knew many young lawyers who were settling in and around Capitol Hill. The narrow brick town houses, shoulder to shoulder, with their long flights of stairs, were as unlike the dwelling places I knew as they could be. Many were painted. They were white or cream, pale blue, a reddish pink. I loved their miniature iron gates and bay windows, their vertical coziness, which spoke, ultimately, not of life at home but of a life looking outward to the drama of the city. The public spaces were grand, numerous, and constantly calling. A person bewitched by politics had no need of a large living room. There were parties and receptions to go to.

The eighties had begun. On the Hill, fitful gentrification was under way. Too near what were considered dangerous neighborhoods, many of the town houses had been crumbling for years. But now some were being restored. Others, purchased with a speculative eye and still shabby, were being rented out to the young professionals just beginning their careers or being sold to them as condominiums.

Only a few blocks from the town house where my boyfriend lived was a gourmet shop that sold jelly beans, Ronald Reagan's favorite snack. They were bite-sized, similar to those in the nickel machine at the barber's back home, where Charlie got his crew cuts. But whereas the barber shop jelly beans were a standard mix (cherry, lemon, lime), the beans made in honor of Ronald Reagan came in a bountiful array of exotic flavors and colors—strawberry, daiquiri, pear, watermelon, coconut, root beer, blueberry, popcorn, tangerine. Add to this gourmet coffee beans, assorted cheeses, sauces, dips, and baked goods. What a world it was and would be for those lucky enough to live along the Northeast Corridor!

As long as Washington got some snow in winter, and I had seen that it did, it seemed a potential home (although the summer heat, billowing with moisture, presented a difficult compromise). I could ride the clean new subway cars, read *The Washington Post,* wear navy blue dresses and matching pumps. Maybe Grover would buy a town house or part of one. Maybe I could help him fix it up and fill it with nice things prettily arranged. He would need Oriental rugs, paintings in gold frames, and his law school diploma on the wall. It would all be correct but with a youthful contemporary flair.

I got a summer job there. One night, Grover's roommate, Mickey, and I sat talking in their living room. Grover lay in bed upstairs where an old air-conditioner rattled. I liked Mickey; he was funny and open, the least impressed with his own Harvard Law School credentials of anyone I had met there. We sat up worrying what to do for a person determined to sweat out something that seemed more than a stomachache.

In the morning Grover assented to calling a doctor and was ordered to come in. His pain by now was so intense that I was to drive him in his car. It was my first time behind the wheel, ever, on the East Coast. Under any other circumstances, I would have refused. My experience was the long straight two-lane highways of the prairie states, where another car was a welcome diversion. My experience was on broad Main Streets with angle parking, in quiet neighborhoods where everyone drove slowly and came to a full stop at the corner. It was in a place where the stretch of highway that ran through town was referred to as the four-lane, so noteworthy did it seem that we had risen to this level of vehicular activity. (The four-lane became a two-lane once you left town.)

Grover and I set out, with Grover in the passenger seat, in pain. The rotaries came at me as though Pierre L'Enfant had planned them with my personal extinction in mind. I did not know when it was my turn to go, which lane to take in, which to take out.

"Watch out!" Grover cried, surfacing from his pain, not knowing which of two deaths he might face. He tried to give me directions. I trembled, crazed with adrenaline. Today, I do not know where the doctor's office was or how we got there. Grover went in and came out. The pain was making him cry, which embarrassed him. Shortly we were in a room at GW Hospital, to which we walked. The doctor had felt Grover's abdomen, diagnosed appendicitis, and ordered surgery.

In the hospital room I went soggy with tears.

Grover looked at me with annoyance, pointing out that he was the one in trouble. Soon he was in bed, drowsing in the deep peace of painkillers.

Mickey arrived. We talked about how doctors and nurses could make mistakes. This hospitalization was up to us, we realized, to two friends of the patient, including one who could barely drive and had only just recently quit crying. We were going to have to pay attention, we agreed; we were going to have to be advocates. We found the doctor and asked questions. We were twenty-five.

Grover's father flew in.

The gesture seemed fitting and dramatic. It was exactly the kind of drama my own family did not go in for. *Get me on the next flight!* My parents would never say that. My parents had to get the paper out.

Grover's father was a steel-company executive. He wore good suits and took flights all the time. When he appeared in the hospital corridor, I knew my part was done. First, I was merely weak with gratitude. Then I felt awe: I could not have been more dazzled if I had seen some ancient kingly beast, reassembled bone by bone and filling a pilastered hall at the Smithsonian.

The father had been a college football star, known, because of his speed, as the Bullet. He had risen from modest origins in coal country and now was in charge of things, the kind of guy who got relocated to solve steel-company problems. It was not hard to see, in Grover, the drive that had been passed on. The only son among a brood of girls, Grover had barreled through college in three years, claimed a top position on the law review, and landed a Supreme Court clerkship. Now the source of all this stood with us, alert, confident, and ready to make progress.

The transfer of power was as orderly as at any inaugural. Mickey and I let ourselves become the kids. The Bullet took charge. I leaned on his plucky cheer, which emerged after he had satisfied himself that all was in order. He took us to dinner and I ate greedily after hours of not having done so. I felt guilty enjoying the food, being healthy, while Grover suffered.

At some point during the hours that were not hours but only a kind of shared fearful space, Grover was borne off in a cloud of scrubbed competence. Using a sharp blade made of excellent steel, someone cut into his abdomen and removed his appendix. When he came to, he asked when they were going to start.

Grover's appendix, the doctor said, had been a nine and a half on a scale of ten. Who knew how soon it might have burst? I shuddered with the sense of calamity narrowly averted.

The recovery took several days. Grover's father remained for one day but then had to go.

"Don't leave," I wanted to plead. I wanted to throw myself at his feet, wrap my arms around his knees.

It was years before I realized that it was really him I needed in those days—that it was the father I had been seeking in Grover. I needed a father's gifts of strength and assurance, transferred in regular jolts like caffeine. Grover, burdened with sky-high standards of attainment, needed all his strength for himself.

I do not blame either of us now for taking so long to grow up. That is the system in this country, especially for those of whom much is expected. School and more school. Killing competitions for grades and distinction. Years of financial dependence. We are not supposed to have much pity for the nation's rootless, driven young. Look at their chances; look at their hopes. But I say look at the scarring. Look how lonely it all was.

Some days passed and then Grover was out of the hospital, back at his clerk's desk wasting no time.

"Who was Savonarola?" the justice quizzed. "What did Kant say in his *Critique of Pure Reason*?"

The hours were long.

I made white wine spritzers with the wife of Grover's co-clerk, read Proust, cleaned Grover and Mickey's freezer, which contained several packages of half-used hamburger buns. Too soon, it was time to take the train back north.

A couple of months after Grover's surgery, Ronald Reagan was shot. I watched on TV as they took him straight to GW Hospital. I knew that front entrance, those shabby, ill-lit corridors. The place was in drastic need of a makeover. Surely there should be something better for a president.

I was in Providence, finishing what would be my last year of a graduate program and trying to write a novel about South Dakota. It did not sound like Tolstoy. It did not sound like anybody's idea of a novel. Still, I had returned from my summer job in Washington with relief. The city had felt, in the end, dangerous, cut in two by race and simmering with rage. A short time into my stay I saw a black man being chased through a grocery store one Sunday by a white guard with a gun. On Capitol Hill one evening, a black youth threw a bottle at Grover and me and another couple as we were returning from a Mexican restaurant. We stared in shock as the bottle shattered at our feet.

All summer Grover was having coughing fits he could not stop. Mickey and I did not know whether to try the Heimlich Maneuver, and we were not quite sure how to do it anyway. One night it got so bad I called 911. The fit subsided. The rescuers were nice about it and tried to assure me I had done the right thing, though Grover did not think so; he was embarrassed. The day before I returned to Providence, someone was murdered in Alexandria, in the fun and fancy historical part only a few blocks from where I lived.

Reagan, of course, was fine and as firm a supporter of the right to bear arms as ever. His wife, Nancy, even said that she carried a little teeny gun herself, right in her purse. No one with any power had a word to say about race or poverty, the city's undercurrent of despair. The jelly bean presidency resumed. My heart sang to be out of there.

The general spruce-up did not stop. In D.C., nice restaurants were opening up on the Hill, little romantic places that served duck and Dover sole and had fresh roses and hunting prints in their tiny bathrooms. More town houses went condo. The prices were going up and up, and people were warned to take the leap before it was too late. Everyone went out for Sunday brunch and got croissant flakes all over their copies of *The New York Times*.

I came down on the train during vacation breaks. Things were good, were going to be ever so much better, for the young lawyers and lobbyists and aides starting out on Capitol Hill. Everyone felt it. I knew a couple, still in their twenties, who had already bought a place and were filling it with wonderful things: a baby grand piano, an antique brass daybed where a guest could sleep under a huge down comforter. "Hitching our little wagon to inflation," they beamed with irony. They were fearsomely bright, wickedly funny, every bit each other's equal. They were also profoundly unsentimental. I think they knew better than most what kind of ride the country was on in those days.

The boy who threw the bottle at us that night also knew, and his message was plain. He had as little to do with a Kahlua-flavored jelly bean as a cow has to do with Jupiter. Existentially, boy and bean were not even in the same universe. The Reagan Revolution, I suspected, was not for everyone. And maybe it was not for me.

I did not move to Washington. I could not find a job there and was not exactly sorry. Providence, Rhode Island, was where I found a job, at the newspaper. For the first time I would have a wage I could live on. The salary, around $18,000, seemed huge. I could not believe anyone would give me so much.

I found a one-bedroom apartment with pristine white walls, tall windows, and refinished floors. It was my fifth living space since leaving college. There, I had lived in a different room, different building, each year. Four different homes. A total of nine places I had tried to decorate, to make my own, since leaving the Dutch colonial on Sixth Street.

In Providence, I could not seem to get the boxes open and start again. I sensed it meant leaving Grover.

Building a home takes so long. It is assembled piece by piece: rug, bed, couch. Even with these staples, an apartment may rattle with emptiness, almost the way it does when you first inspect it and imagine yourself there with your things. And yet you are always on your way out of an apartment, from the day you haul in the first box and tell yourself a tale of permanence so that you will have the strength to unpack.

For my newspaper job, I needed a car. Day by day I learned to drive it in Rhode Island's gnarly and impatient traffic. I stopped trying to go the speed limit the first week, after I understood what universal hostility this evoked. I learned the highways and the route numbers and the exits, but I did not get used to any of it for a long time. On weekends I was grateful to park my car and do everything I needed to do on foot, as I had always done before, in Boston, in Washington, as a student in Providence.

Grover and I parted. I became an official single woman. I moved through the days with an uneasy, unrelenting sense that I was doing something women were not supposed to do. The punishments for being without the protection of a man included exploitation by landlords and repairmen; break-ins; the constant threat of rape, or rape deluxe, which included being grievously wounded and left for dead.

How was a single woman supposed to rearrange furniture or haul a table up the stairs? Who would take a single woman to the airport or the doctor if she could not, for some reason, take herself? I was in a permanent state of transgression. I was going to get it for sure. I had one eye on God at all times.

I lived in my new home—which turned into multiple homes, a series of apartments—lightly, provisionally, as if at any moment some angel of the lord might kick in the door and announce: "This is not it at all." I would have cancer or be killed by someone angry about the Reagan Revolution. Or I might not be home at all and, rather, be slammed into on the highway by somebody drunk.

Or maybe it would not be any of these ways, but instead I would finish my days as the single teachers of Plainville had—in homes that were never really home, tidy rooms with things that were not quite right, never quite coordinated because of course you cannot choose carpeting or kitchen cabinets in a place that is not yours. I would be done in, ultimately, by genteel shabbiness, by a kind of smallness I had not foreseen. Mine would be a diminished life. An imitation at-homeness would be my portion, for a sin I could never quite figure out.

Gradually, during these months of general dread, I recovered the pleasures of solitude. I had known them in childhood when in an empty house in summer I would play alone with my horses, preferring this to going in search of a game in progress or attending the summer recreation program at the park.

Mom and Dad were at work; Charlie was off somewhere with his friends. On the square tiles of the apartment floor, I lined up the horses and spun a numbered dial borrowed from a board game, advancing the horses in turn, seeing which would win the race.

In Providence, the rituals of solitude came to include a book or movie on tape, a fresh bunch of tulips, a glass of wine, chocolate truffles, a bubble bath, a new compact disk. Sometimes I lay on the floor listening to Bill Evans spill his yearnings onto the keyboard.

There was a period of patchwork quilt making, the haze of pleasure that went with Christmas gift wrapping, or with simply rearranging loved objects on top of the dresser. A whole-apartment cleaning binge could end in pulsing satisfaction, as could the neatening of files and drawers, and the resolute purging from time to time of objects that no longer appealed to me or had lost their usefulness.

All of these things could have been done with others present. But alone, I felt an intensity of focus and a stretching amplitude of self that never came in spaces shared with others. Minus the givens of my various apartments (wall colors, for instance, or kitchen flooring) everything around me was something I had deliberately chosen. My preoccupations and pleasures spoke through objects. The apartments I inhabited were a sequence of symbolic universes in which, say, the catalogue from the latest art exhibit held prominent place, evoking images just seen. Or it might be souvenirs from my latest journey or even my latest shopping excursion. The just-purchased sweater or candle would sit out, refreshing my eye, enlivening my home with a sense of the new.

Over time I built a whole vocabulary of pleasures and meaning from a world that, as a child, I had only been able to imagine as unbearably diminished. But attention to the orderliness and harmony of my surroundings was not all; freedom of mind, a form of domestic meditation, overlay the satisfactions of dwelling alone in a place. I would begin to read, and my mind would depart from the text, roaming over lush new terrain. My eye might stop at a vase of dried roses or study the objects on my writing desk: a green shell, an apothecary jar filled with pencils. I would contemplate the light: limpid frankness in winter, a saturating glare in July. The music I played might unexpectedly evoke some past experience, and I would retrieve the thing whole, savoring the details, and wondering anew at the power of loss to exalt the ordinary. It was years before I understood that I was lonely; my aloneness was so rich.

Did Tolstoy long to please? I wonder. I doubt it. At least he could not have done so in the way of young women. It is only in solitude—free of the need to respond to anyone else, free of enslavement to approval—that young women get an inkling of who they are. The pleasures of the world appear to them in full. They recognize Being. All the Pentecost a girl could ever want waits for her in a one-bedroom apartment.

If I had been Milton, *Paradise Lost* would contain an angel who drags Eve up to a pine-fragrant mountaintop and shows her the thrilling vein of women's solitariness: a sapphire stream of gorgeous angles so far below it is all but hidden. These are waters that lie far from men. I found them by accident and will forever be grateful.

During my years in Providence, I lived in six apartments. Rent increases, obtuse landlords, noisy neighbors, and the simple hope for better kept me on the move. Of these, it was the most beautiful one that got broken into. It had white walls with a faint hint of pink, a fireplace with a classic white mantelpiece flanked by two window seats. Above these were two matching stained-glass windows with a rose design. There were bay windows in the living room and dining room and a built-in china cabinet with leaded-glass doors.

The apartment was on the first floor. I took it as though in a trance, on the wings of an observation made once by my married friend Voltaire. It was only when you were on the first floor, she said, that you could feel anything like a real sense of home. The couple who had the apartment before me assured me they had not had a bit of trouble security-wise. They showed me the small wooden blocks they had made that screwed into the window frames, preventing the windows from being opened too far from the outside. They left the blocks with me.

The first break-in was in July. I came home from my shift as a night editor to find the back door bolted against me. Slow to understand, I tried again and again with the key. Then, shaking, I went to the front door, and let myself in. The stereo was gone. The bedroom had been ransacked; a window gaped open. A box of photographs was on the bed, moved from its shelf in the closet. Someone had gone through the pictures, looked over my life. The jewelry box was missing several items: some inexpensive earrings, the charm bracelet for which I had walked around and around the table that summer my family drove west.

The next night, almost without a word, three other single women from the copy desk came home with me, and we sat together through the hour of three A.M.—the hour at which the threat of night seems to soften, and turn. By four the promised safety of daylight seems at hand.

We talked about work and our lives and ate slices of the Bundt cake the robbers had unaccountably left undisturbed on the counter the night before. Why had they not stolen the cake? It looked so prim, sitting there in the midst of my shredded safety zone. *Come on in! Set a spell!* Sometimes a tornado will sheer off a roof and leave a doily precisely in place.

My married landlords, tucked safely on the second floor, disagreed with my request for bars on the bedroom windows, even though these windows were hidden from the street. They said they disliked the aesthetics. They proposed, instead, small window fans. But I had read of a recent burglary in which an entire air conditioner was removed.

I bought the most beautiful curtains I could find—white panels trimmed in lace—for the bedroom. Beauty, of course, is no weapon against intruders—from then on, I slept with the fireplace poker within reach—but it can hold down the fear. The curtains were the only way I knew to rebuild my relationship with the room. For months I could not stop picturing the open window, the entry point, symbol of violation.

Women are permitted no escape from the imagery of vulnerability. I got it, all right: hardy har har. During the daytime I was full of irony and jokes; in the dark I was silent and alert, weighing every noise, a light sleeper. The insect zapper in the next yard sounded like the foot of a man breaking a twig.

In imagination I heard frontier voices. I pictured myself rocking silently in the dark in my beautiful two-bedroom, a shotgun on my lap. *We're stayin'! Never mind your plagues of locusts, your wild savage war parties, cattle rustlers, and horse thieves. We're whippin' up a mess of biscuits. Go tell Aunt Rhody.*

The second break-in was a daytime one, also in summer. The thieves must have used a crowbar. They pulled a study window completely out of its frame, after discovering that they could not open it wide enough past the wooden block to get in. (In the first break, my window had been closed and locked, but the screw-block was not in place.)

After I returned from the laundromat to discover the second break-in, my friend Emerald came right over. Her hands were covered with white paint from the bookcase she was refinishing.

She stayed with me for much of the afternoon as I raged, as fear fanned my heart. As *We're stayin'!* became *We're goin'!*

I would have to move, I knew, to the fortified higher ground where single women belonged. One break-in was a mystery. Two were a message. I found a tiny place in a brick apartment building that had been fixed up and was going condo. (Rent to own! the landlord kept urging, even as he failed to fill the oil tank.)

My new place was a one-bedroom with barely enough room to turn around. Once again I was on the third floor. The third floor was becoming my default position. My friends came over and stared solemnly around, snaking their way through the boxes. This was no home, they knew. I knew it too. I set up the bed, threw the deadbolts, and slept deeply for the first time in two years.

One Thanksgiving Day, when Emerald's small house was broken into—the one she bought by herself and restored, unearthing its Greek Revival dignity from a chaos of linoleum and stained wallpaper—it was I who made the discovery, who went sick at the sight of shattered glass, who listened as Emerald vowed to move to Maine. Instead, she got an unlisted phone number (her break-in was the experiment-in-terror kind, followed up by phone calls from someone who addressed her by name). She installed window bars and a series of locks that would foil Houdini. It all held up against the next attempt. The shattered glass next to the door, a repeat of the first-time strategy, was as far as the intruder got.

Emerald stayed. She applied for a plaque designating her house's historic pedigree. When you visit, you can read the plaque as you listen to the series of locks clicking open. You wait on the stone steps, circa 1848, and listen to the sounds of modern security. Inside are flowers and candles in honor of a birthday, or you follow a cluttered route to the back and cocktails in the tiny garden. Every year Emerald's house seemed mysteriously to expand, accommodating dogs and cats, artwork and dishes, new treasures Emerald had dragged back from secondhand shops. A growing roster of alumni who inhabited the small apartment upstairs remembers her with cards, visits, gifts of food and cat toys in an implausible upending of the usual landlord-tenant relationship. The gods say what they say. Meanwhile, Emerald has built a tiny fortification in a narrow lane, and it is stuffed with life.

Providence, Rhode Island. The oddness of it. The unlikelihood.

It was in Providence that I met Andrew, after years of single life and dateless Daughter of Job weekends. One evening at Leo's, the bar everybody went to and I usually avoided, he simply appeared. Introduced to me as a sculptor, he was a friend of friends, a child of Rhode Island known to them for years.

At the next table, the governor was braying about various issues and hoping to be noticed. Andrew and I talked about the Rodin Museum in Paris, which we had both visited. After missing each other there, we had kept it up in Rhode Island: For the last three years, Andrew had been away at graduate school in Indiana. He said the Midwest was the most exotic place he could think of to go. Now he was back.

In the years just after college, Providence had not been a part of my mental terrain at all. I bobbed from Boston to New York to Washington and back, looking for the business of my life along the Northeast Corridor. I had clutched my purse at Penn Station, sat quietly in the prayerful silence at New Haven, where they changed engines. Providence was just a place I passed through. Looking from the window, I could not tell what it was like.

Gritty, probably. Minor. The people who boarded the train there had the vague humility of a farm team in baseball.

I could see dull-looking buildings on the hill. On the other side of the tracks was Rhode Island's state house, a pile of white marble that seemed overdone compared with its red-brick counterpart in Boston.

Back and forth I went, taking little notice of Providence until I was accepted into a master's degree program there. Before I said yes, I wanted a look. Meg said she would like to see Providence too and on one of her days off drove me down from Boston. We parked next to an imposing Georgian brick mansion and studied its broad lawn, enclosed by an extravagance of cream-colored pickets.

Space. A sloping prairie that rolled straight into our hearts and carried us home. Meg read the sign—JOHN BROWN HOUSE—and broke into song: "John Brown had a little Indian," retrieving a childhood ditty I had not thought of in years as easily as if she were pulling a peanut butter sandwich from her knapsack.

One little two little three little Indians . . .

To me, school was a treacherous proving ground, and so I was anxious. But the Brown campus meant no such thing to Meg. It was spring and whatever was flowering made the air smell like licorice. We strolled through and identified the campus green. It was nice here, far less congested than in Cambridge, pretty. Brown was surrounded by block after block of carefully tended historic houses. We walked past them in amazement. Someone had forgotten to wreck this place.

It was possible, I knew, even before my chat with the dean. I could come here. I could walk out of my rent-controlled Cambridge bunker and surrender to something easier. I could live in Providence.

. . .

In my memory, it is as though that was the last time I saw Meg before she moved back home. Our day in Providence was a good day with perfect weather. We wandered along Thayer Street and looked in the shops. We had a nice lunch. When we got back to Boston we had the satisfied sense of having been away to some-place pleasant. Everything seemed better.

When she gave up on Boston, Meg went to Minneapolis first—the best idea a person from the upper Midwest has for fix-ing her life. In winter the tall glass buildings flush rosy at dawn, look like upright ice palaces. In summer they remind you of a cool drink. Meg was not there for long before she decided to marry the beau she had left behind and move with him to San Antonio. All over America, nurses were needed. Meg could go anywhere. She told me her plan in a long-distance phone call to-ward the end of my time at Brown. I happened to be in a strange mood. That day I believed suddenly, fervently, that we could get what we wanted. I did not know how Meg's decision fit with my revelation though. Our hopes and fears collided over the wires in one big messy turning point. Meg seemed completely peaceful, the way I was that day I could not find an apartment, found blood on my foot, and decided to move back home.

"When will my real life begin?" Meg was always asking, feeling what I felt during our Boston time. Day after day we descended into one subway stop and emerged from another. Where was home? Where was the situation that would hold us for a life-time—the great love or cause?

One day it simply ended. But I did not feel the door close until a few years later, after I was installed in Providence and had begun working for the paper. From time to time I would go to Boston for the day. On one of these occasions I was waiting at the Park Street stop. A young man with a guitar sang: "It's gonna take a lot of love . . . to get us through the night." It was an old song. At one time you heard it everywhere. The singer's voice, slow and wispy, reached only a handful of people. The sound bounced off the tiles of the subway station the way light does at an indoor swimming pool. Then the train came, rattling along toward its crescendo, toward arrival, which sounds exactly like a bowling ball hitting every single pin: a clean strike. The doors of the cars jerked open. People rushed out, rushed in. In an instant, we were gone.

One more memory of Boston: I am two years out of college and have been working downtown at a publishing house. It is a nice day in late spring, and Meg comes to meet me for lunch. She will spend the day going to movies and window shopping. It is her day off, a whole sweet day of doing whatever she wishes, of being young, of having great hopes.

We find a sunny spot on the Common, on a slope. It is as though we can see the Common's whole broad dangerous exhilarating stretch, the tall buildings far beyond, the stately brick structures closer by, lining the Beacon Hill side. We eat bag lunches and then blow bubbles from the plastic bottle Meg has brought.

The bubbles are familiar. Sometimes these bottles with the plastic wand inside were given out as favors at birthday parties we attended as children. They cost ten cents then. In Cambridge, taxi drivers—Ph.D.s run aground—often carry them, blowing bubbles from the window and thinking of William James as they wait for a fare.

As in childhood, Meg and I are waiting for our adult lives to start. Maybe they will start this very afternoon. Whom will we marry? How many children, what kind of house and car? We are dying of suspense. Our actual terrestrial location is Boston Common. But this is simultaneously one of the long dreamy Barbie days on Sixth Street. Before us is another summer to fill. We do not mind the wait. We look at the people on the Common, at the blue sky, at the bubbles floating away. We would not move on for anything.

ROYAL COPENHAGEN

GRANDMA TAIT looked at dishes. All the women in our family looked at dishes. If they happened to go into the jewelry store for any reason, they looked at the new designs of fine china offered to brides. Which one? Which set would you choose for happily ever after? Idly I would pick because I had been brought along, because there was nothing else to do. In spring, place settings were displayed in the Plainville store's window with the names of the couples who had chosen them written elegantly on a card.

I supposed it was possible that one day I would care about dishes. But I preferred looking at horses—toy or TV or real. I did not get the idea of dishes. "It's a dish," I wanted to say. "It's not even the main part of the meal. That would be the food."

One summer day late in the eighties, Emerald and I rode the train from Stockholm to Copenhagen. The trip took all day. But in summer Scandinavia features hour after hour of daylight, and we did not feel tired. When we arrived, we went straight to our hotel, checked in, dumped our bags, and set off on foot for Royal

Copenhagen, the mother store of one of the finest porcelain makers in the world. We made it before closing time. We had time to spare. We had been traveling in Scandinavia for two weeks, and every minute of that time, we were on our way to Royal Copenhagen.

What is the logic of loving dishes? I can see none. I suppose I began to take an interest just after college, when I was first trying to build a home around myself. Geographically speaking, every place I landed was foreign. But dwelling spaces were another matter. I had little control over basic elements such as window treatments or flooring. But with dishes I could express a preference, exclude all other choices. Here is my home: Look, these are the cups I picked out. If you changed apartments, your dishes, vessels of familiarity, came along with you.

Women dreaming over place settings in the bridal registry section of the china shop are up to something more. They savor the notion of a fresh start, imagine a home in which only an idea of the present is expressed, and everything distasteful that has accumulated in their lives is omitted. Objects from other times, from faulty ideas of the beautiful, or objects merely acquired by necessity, fall away under this bridal gaze, whether the woman is sixteen or sixty. Likewise family tensions disperse. In the home where everything is new, everything is harmony.

Royal Copenhagen offers three classic patterns, all easily recognizable in its signature blue and white. I did go through a blue and white period in my Cambridge apartment (white Haitian cotton love seat; blue clock and blue wooden candlestick; a seascape complete with gull to flesh out what I dreamed I saw when looking out the window). But it was not the traditional colors that accounted for my fascination with Royal Copenhagen. Rather, at the time of our trip, I had become interested in my Danish origins and therefore in all things Danish. Owing to Dad, I was half Danish. Royal Copenhagen china was one of the things the Danes made, and so it had something to do with him and with me. Once there were Viking ships; now these dishes were the Danes' gift to the world.

What I was not prepared for were the sensations of familiarity that washed over me at every turn as soon as we reached Denmark. I saw women with high foreheads and fine hair like mine; men with noses like Dad's (and mine). I saw the sharp chin passed on to some of Niels Ebbesen Hansen's grandchildren. Our train conductor had the generic look of a high school band director from any South Dakota town. Trucks went by that said "Andersen" on the side. The Copenhagen phone book was full of Andersens. I would not have any struggle here, as I so often had at home, to get my name spelled right. Not Anderson! At last what I was was right.

I glided through Copenhagen with a feeling of physical accord. On a crowded street, a child singled me out and asked the time in Danish. I had long chats (in English) with record store salesmen about jazz; babbled to waiters about Isak Dinesen and open-faced sandwiches; was amazed to hear the same intake of breath with the word *ya* that I had heard on the prairie. I had the feeling we all knew the same jokes—that the dry humor binding Dad's relatives had fermented here. I felt dead certain that no harm could come to me in Denmark.

Reason, the great spoiler, suggested that what I felt was surely illusion. But as long as we were at it, reason also urged me to check out a human tendency I had believed I was exempt from. I apprehended at last, and I think truly for the first time, the tribalism lurking in our chemistry.

To be among one's own kind! To be so thoroughly and deeply recognized—so like the others. Is this not what we mean, above all, when we speak of home? This fierce clinging of the spirit to the group, to the dream of the group, has popped up all over the world at all times. Now it was I who felt its giddy pleasures.

Alas, as we all well know, it was the dream of the group that delivered the twentieth century into its distinguishing conflagration. My delight was mixed with regret. It was necessary, I saw, to keep some distance from these beguiling feelings. But it was not easy. When the Nazis occupied their land during the Second World War, the Danes knew they were overmatched. And so they offered cagey resistance. When Danish Jews were ordered to identify themselves by wearing the Star of David, all the Danes put one on. After the war, plaques went up on various farmhouses, almost all of them white stucco with dark thatched roofs. HERE PAULSEN AND NIELSEN WERE SHOT FOR HIDING JEWS, the plaques read.

I tried not to feel proud. I reminded myself that (a) I was only half Dane and (b) I personally had done nothing to aid the war effort; I had not even been born in time. More important (c) I am timid. I am not courageous at all. At the slightest threat, I twist my lion's tail and quake. The most that could be said of me is that I am stubborn. "Stubborn Danes," Dad used to say absently, in a way that mystified me but that now seemed slightly clearer. They were that, these Danes. Never mind Hitler; they were going to do what was right if it killed them. I pictured them making some crack, unable to resist, even as they were being lined up against the white wall. *Careful, Herr Schmidt, we just had this painted last week.*

I was not there only to seek my heritage. In some sense I was also looking for Kierkegaard. A famous statue of him was not far from our hotel, and we made a pilgrimage there. It was a pilgrimage of self-conscious irony: When we saw the statue, we laughed. Weren't we there, really, for the pleasures of the city? We had arrived in the midst of a jazz festival and kept stumbling across wonderful performers playing free of charge in assorted public squares. The June air was as fresh as clean laundry. We dined on expertly prepared salmon and cucumber salads. And we were having the time of our life in the shops. What was the sense of Kierkegaard's brooding presence in a city such as this?

I had long felt that I did not get Kierkegaard. But I wanted to. At some level I did not fully admit to myself, I sensed he could help corral the red balloon I had lost that day in the Princeton chapel. Kierkegaard might be the thinking woman's guide to belief.

Kierkegaard's lifelong tussle with Christianity and with feelings that had no home in church dogma made sense to me. But in reading him, I could never see what his conclusion was. I had only a shaky understanding of existentialism and of why Kierkegaard was referred to as an exponent. Perhaps of most interest, his anxieties seemed historically premature. They held their small stage from 1813 to 1855—before the U.S. Civil War; before Emerson, in America, had worked himself into his trademark optimistic froth.

Kierkegaard went at the established Christian church like a battering ram. But even more so, he went at God, which is what every anxious person has done since the Enlightenment. Provided for by his father's fortune, Kierkegaard could worry about God full time. He had an incapacity to let the matter drop. What is a Christian? How shall we live and what for? His journals probing such questions were voluminous. Books that defied categorization poured forth. They were part tract, part personal confession, part fiction.

Despite all the words he put down, however, Kierkegaard may be most famous for a single act: his renunciation of Regine.

Regine was the great love of Kierkegaard's youth. No other came along. His decision not to marry has been read as the most momentous turn of his life, and yet who can trust it? Kierkegaard implies he was saving himself for some higher aim. But what? Reading him, we are stuck with this thwarted, unreliable narrator and an image of Regine, poor Regine, who married someone else but surely wondered her whole life: Was it me?

Kierkegaard's love of renunciation went only so far. Like Tolstoy in his later years, Kierkegaard believed in the ascetic life. But he could not quite bring himself to practice it. He enjoyed living well and zestfully worked his way through the money left by his father. Years ago I read that he had a special fondness for teacups (Emerald said she could identify) and collected them. But I have not been able to find the reference since then. When he died, in his early forties, Kierkegaard was carrying home the last of his cash. The friends and relatives who closed out his affairs found thirty bottles of wine in the house.

In youth Kierkegaard had been estranged from his father. But the father finally reeled him in, confessing to a boyhood act of blasphemy and to a pervasive sense of guilt stemming from sex. This act of confiding moved Kierkegaard to a new devotion. Proof of his father's love raised the parallel possibility that God's paternal love was also real. And thus, according to one view, arose Kierkegaard's primary insight: Life in the world is a form of homesickness. And home is the love of the father. Kierkegaard's perception came on a trip to his father's literal homeland, the province of Jutland, in 1840. As it happens, and if the family historians are correct, my fatherland is the same.

. . .

After Emerald and I had had our fill of Copenhagen, we planned to go north to the tip of Denmark, where two seas meet. They are the North Sea and the Kattegat. In the nineteenth century, painters gathered in this region, in the area called Skagen, to consider the singular light. To get there, we took a ferry to Jutland, the largest piece of Denmark (and, some have said, the most Danish). Jutland juts up like a thumb, with Skagen at the top.

We stationed ourselves on the open upper deck, where we could gaze into the Danish sea. The ferry was full of families going to Legoland, the amusement park built around another of Denmark's famous products—Legos, the interlocking plastic blocks made in primary colors and exported to children all over the world.

The boat contained a roomy play area. It was attractive and clean. We marveled, not for the first time, at how generously and without fuss the Danes incorporated children into their public spaces; at how much they genuinely seemed to like children. *Bairn* they call them; the word seems so much more tender than *children,* with its harsh opening consonant and stiff syllables. *Children:* an English word direct from the joyless lips of the governess. *Children* implies a world of duty and self-denial in which pleasure is permitted only at the margins, the world of my California cousins.

Ever on guard against romantic illusions about the Danes, Emerald and I both watched for bratty behavior among the children on board. But we saw little. The people on the ferry seemed to be taking a calm, almost reverent pleasure in the light, whose duration that day would reach past suppertime, beyond nine o'clock. It would lengthen even more as we traveled north.

When Jutland came into view, I held myself in suspense. What did I feel? My father's father's branch was said to have begun here.

Emerald and I even planned a pass through Løgstør, believed to be my ancestral hometown. I focused on the landscape, trying to memorize details.

Jutland was flat, dun-colored terrain verging on a cold sea. It looked harsher than Zealand, the green fairyland from which we had just come. Except for the water, it looked (surprise surprise) like the Midwestern prairie.

The ferry docked, and we retrieved our rental car from the lower deck. As we drove farther into Jutland and away from the coast, I felt uncannily oriented. It seemed as though we were traveling through the farmland near Grandma and Grandpa Andersen's house in South Dakota. I even felt a familiar upwelling of boredom, the kind associated with long childhood trips past infinite fields, where there was so little for the eye to seize on. The ear was also tested. In their valiant struggle for material, radio announcers on the prairie would report hog prices and upcoming sales at forgettable stores. They would tell the starting times of church suppers and 4-H meetings, whose anniversaries were being celebrated, and which couples requested no gifts.

Yet these associations did not weigh on my spirits. Instead I felt a pleasurable connection, as though a simple familiar melody had been presented with more interesting chords and in a new, more pleasing key. Here was my home terrain. But in Denmark, it had historical depth, cultural richness, and the aesthetic salvation that comes from both. The farmhouses with thatched roofs were satisfying to see. So were the winding roads of the towns, their old churches and half-timbered dwelling places holding sway at the center.

Why do the human habitations of my home state so often lack

charm? The old dwellings, classic frame houses painted white, are typically left to rot. Or they are knocked down altogether and replaced by ranch-style houses in dismaying pastels. Ceramic figures crowd the lawn in a themeless frenzy: Elves, deer, and the Virgin Mary keep company with wooden daisies and windmills. Sometimes the old houses are left up and hideously added on to. Classic barns are replaced or supplemented with low-slung prefabricated structures. The outskirts of towns are thronged with new cheaply constructed buildings, grimly functional, while stately old buildings on Main Street are left to molder. Often, these suffer a procession of eager but ineffectual low-margin tenants: a hair salon; a crafts shop; a photo studio.

It was not that Denmark lacked such expediencies. Downtown Løgstør had a practical Midwestern air, and I bought Danish flag stickers in what seemed to be Løgstør's equivalent of Stemsrud's dime store. But older structures remained and had been treated with care. A discerning eye was at work, along with affection for the public square.

Too often, newness is the only aesthetic criterion applied in the Midwest. Newer is better (and also cheaper). The old is too much trouble. The biggest question that enters in is whether it is easy to park in a place. And that usually means another vote for the new.

These concerns Kierkegaard would have categorized as aesthetic, though he meant far more by the term than the looks of a place. The aesthetic for Kierkegaard was a sphere of existence, exemplified by the romantic writers. There were two other spheres, the ethical and the religious. (Notice the creeping trinitarianism?) Kierkegaard readers want to know: Are the spheres mutually exclusive or may they intersect? Are the three modes of existence more properly stages, with the religious, if you reach it, the highest and best?

From what I can tell, Kierkegaard embraced the aesthetic mode as a young man. He was going to be a writer. He would live and love and write. He would eat well, go to concerts and the theater. And then he would write.

It turned out not to be enough.

Kierkegaard began to criticize the Romantics, rejecting their project as doomed. Beneath Romanticism's intoxication, he found, was a series of trapdoors that went from doubt to despair. And so Kierkegaard moved on. He conceived no lyric poems, no farces, no heroes in a bind. For Kierkegaard there was only the bind of the soul. He weighed the soul's every impulse, dissected its moods, doubted it, scolded it, caressed it. Life and career merged in a dense dream of self-accusation that was obscurely meant, while he was at it, to rebuke all Danes and every soul trained up in Christianity ever after. God was transcendent, beyond our reach, and the only object worthy of desire. Rather than pursue the false satisfactions of beauty, we must build our conveyances—rafts lashed together with rags; mechanical birds made of muslin and feathers—and try to reach him.

Anyone who has gone out for an expensive evening—to dine in candlelight on white linen and afterward to attend a fine performance—knows the sagging heart that was Kierkegaard's subject. We smile at our companion; we are, in some fashion, grateful. Yet the deep interior murmurings—ours alone, it seems—ask why? Why is this beautiful time not enough? Kierkegaard has an answer: Paddle like hell toward the father.

When Emerald and I reached Skagen, we encountered even more light than when we had first reached Jutland. It flooded in, as though from some failed dike in the sky, dousing the land. In a small museum were the paintings, wistful and romantic, composed by those who had come here to work a hundred years before. In one we especially liked, a group of women in long white dresses, some with their hair pulled up from the napes of their necks, walked in an amiable group along the beach. They were surrounded by northern light almost as white as their dresses but tinged with rose.

The next day Emerald and I drove to the exact sands shown in the painting. We stared out at the churning water where the North Sea and the Kattegat collided. They met in a long line of waves resembling the hair on the neck of an angry dog. This was the limit of Denmark, and it was far from tranquil. We wandered on the sand, glad of our denim jackets in the wind, and picked up some of the smallest shells we had ever seen. We were and were not the women in the painting. I did and did not apprehend in the battling seas a metaphor for my soul, the same old clash between the world's delights and the panting after God I kept running into wherever I went. Skagen was Tolstoy all over again.

"Kierkegaard," Emerald said, shaking her head, laughing always at the mere mention of his name. "Kierkegaard and shopping." It had become the implausible theme of our trip.

What, exactly, was I after? I had come to the land of my imagined tribe only to find myself, at odd moments, in pursuit of a philosopher who disdained the herd. "Look at all you are missing," I might have pointed out to him on the ferry ride to Jutland. "Sunshine! The sea! A boat full of genial Danes!" But when the landscape of Jutland finally materialized before him, Kierkegaard saw only his father. The father bore down on him like Abraham and at the last minute stayed his sword.

Are we to be spared then? It is a question Job had, and

Kierkegaard had. It is a question I have. When we go to Kierkegaard, we are looking for clues. We want clues on what kind of home to construct for our thoughts. With his impenetrable paradoxes and gooey theorizing, Kierkegaard seems made for us, the perfect voice for our modern confusion. But he is all journey and no destination, a mental rambler who rarely left home and likewise never arrived there. What could he possibly have said to our young woman in Eastboro, the one who ended her life on the tracks so near my back door? Could he have convinced her that all she needed was a leap of faith? Would she have understood what he meant?

One night not long before leaving Denmark, Emerald and I stayed in a castle that had been converted into an inn. It was not far from Odense, the town where Hans Christian Andersen was born, and where there is a big Hans Christian Andersen museum. They show you the house where he lived as a child. It is basically a bare room, so you must imagine everything.

We were the castle's only guests. The caretaker was a silent, pale young man with black hair, and he had a chubby black dog, Leni. Except for Leni, there was something sinister about the place. It was as though all the Scandinavian gloom that ever was, including Hamlet's edgy discontent, had been quietly ushered to this spot.

We fled into town for dinner and lingered over it as long as we could. Back at the castle, we prepared for bed. Our windowless room was comfortable enough, even cozy, if a little too full of gilded items and brocade. We had our own bath. We wondered if it was our last night in the world, and if so, who would get the things we had bought at Royal Copenhagen. We went to bed resigned, two heroines in the grip of a spell.

When we woke in the morning, we were mildly startled. We agreed that it was a surprise not to have been ax-murdered in the night. Since we had not been, however, we were due for another day of touring. We did not waste time pondering the meaning of the caretaker's malaise. But it stayed with me, stray notes from a funeral march.

The countryside near the castle was lush, fairy-story land. Large trees in full leaf lined the roads. Driving along, in high spirits because of our escape, we were shocked to suddenly come across men in uniform. They walked beside the road toting guns. Soon we came upon transport trucks as well. We had the alarming sensation that we had slid back in time to the war. This was any part of Europe, and this was the war in summer; this was what you would see. I tried imagining what it would be like to be invaded, occupied. The dominant emotion, it seemed to me, would not be fear but sheer surprise.

We learned later that the men we had seen were the Danish equivalent of the National Guard and that they were engaged in a training session. Army men in Fairyland. What did these sons of the ugly duckling have to do with real life, the dreary requirements of national defense? Emerald disapproved: Danes, in her view, did not play with guns.

Yet in the end, neither the brooding caretaker at the castle nor the men on maneuvers seriously marred our illusions. The Danes, their Viking fierceness rounded off over the centuries, lived with a sense of proportion and pleasure that seemed prelapsarian. They lived aesthetically (their accomplishments in design and dance, their fondness for music). They lived ethically. High taxes translated into programs designed for the betterment of all—health care and time off to tend young children. The Danes were earnest doers of global good deeds. They lived, it seemed to me, in precisely the spheres that the afflicted Kierkegaard found so insufficient.

There is more of Kierkegaard in the plains of America, I think, than in Denmark. Maybe Kierkegaard even intuited this on his trip to the exceptional landscape of Jutland—that his true homeland lay in a geography he could only dimly sense and would never see; that despite the comforts he managed to surround himself with in Copenhagen, he would live an unaccommodated life.

As for me, I never felt more at home. *This is the place,* I thought exultantly, whether walking down the sunny streets of Copenhagen or breathing the unburdened air in Skagen. This is it.

We rarely live the life of our dreams. With some effort, I could have moved to Denmark and lived there. And why not, if it made me so happy? Certainly at that time I was miserable in Rhode Island. Why not move to Denmark? I asked myself. But in Denmark, I also wondered, who would my friends be? What could be my work, assuming I could manage the formidable job of finding a job? And how would I get back to the prairie with any regularity?

In the Copenhagen airport, where it was still possible to buy a small piece of Georg Jensen silver before leaving, I thought about home. If only this ideal version of home could also be the real one. What did I have to do with the American experiment? What piece of it so vitally required my presence? The fashionable din about diversity that I was returning to now struck me as static spread from coast to coast. And it was trying everyone's patience. *Your group? What about mine?* The nation that had once agreed on the universal desirability of cowboys now agreed on nothing and seethed with tribal resentments.

I needed this?

When we landed in Boston, Emerald and I were immobilized by dread. By comparison, the castle now seemed no worse than a routine interval in a waiting room. We had been away three weeks—a huge amount of time for us. We had left the strain and fear and incompleteness of our single American lives behind and seen something close to an ideal society. Now what, oh twinkling lights of Boston, familiar capital of our urban selves? And it was familiar—lugubriously so. We clutched our baggage, braced ourselves for rudeness, indifference, the sheer exhausting struggle of the heterogeneous many. Logan Airport felt like the lobby of a movie theater just after you have seen something good. The lobby reminds you that you need to fix the faucet. You think of unpaid bills and unwashed clothes.

The bus to Providence took a long time trundling through the Callahan Tunnel. Sometimes we were stalled for several minutes. Emerald and I did not mind. At the other end we would be pulled out of something satisfyingly eternal, our own adult version of a fairy tale, and dumped back into the stream of our small personal histories.

In time I saw that my desire for Denmark was the desire for home, recast as the dream of the native. It was a lovely trick. In the midst of it sat Kierkegaard weaving his word connections to God, an alien in his own country, an alien to his own soul. Oh that Søren; what a cutup he was. What a cautionary tale.

JERUSALEM

ONE SUMMER day, in the great misery of early adolescence, I happened by the Camerons' house. "Why you're blossoming just like a little peony!" Mrs. Cameron pronounced.

Me? With my unmemorable hair, my glasses, my flat chest, my gladiator legs? I felt a whisper of hope.

In our first spring in Eastboro I went out to plant peonies. I knew nothing about them, only that everyone grew them back home without seeming to try, so how hard could it be? *Be careful where you plant them,* the instructions said, *peonies don't like to be moved.*

Now they tell me.

I looked back on my trail of residences, my long trek toward obscure ends. The boxes packed and unpacked. Self-pity waved its plume at me. I had no excuse for waving back. I was an ordinary castaway of the typically American kind. Regularly on the evening news, it was possible to see parents wailing for their children, sometimes passing them over barbed-wire fences to safety. My life and times flickered with children looking for misplaced mothers, uncles, anyone. Unhoused by civil conflicts, millions young and old lost eyes or limbs or fell to disease in the unsanitary conditions of refugee camps. Or, drained of fight, they simply lay down and politely starved, as relief workers in league with camera operators made another exhausted bid for the world's attention.

Orphans in cheerless barracks were good. But the best material, truffles to newshounds, had to do with families. Gain or loss did not matter. What counted was overflowing emotion. I tried to imagine my own undemonstrative family sucked into a newsworthy predicament—for instance, forced on a long march with what goods we could carry, cans of tuna, a photo album, and Grandma Tait's silver. The big difference, of course, was that we would not all happen to be in the same place if trouble erupted.

The news, it seemed, was this: Wherever great suffering occurred, family and place were rolled into one. The great tragedy of our era was uprooting and separation. But the American variety of this experience largely goes unnoted. Our brand of exile is assumed to be voluntary; our separation from family and place is believed to be freely chosen. The answer to our loneliness is O'Hare Airport at Thanksgiving and bumper stickers advising QUITCHERBITCHIN'.

The Sioux were the original nomads of my native terrain. Assigned plots of land after the settlers invaded, they grew miserable and alien. To a human tuber such as I am, this is close to incomprehensible. To the Sioux, though, the contours of the plain suggested movement. The rolling clouds suggested movement. And who is to say the clouds are not a metaphor for the buffalo, which also moved, mowing their way across the grasslands. If you moved, you could eat. You could survive.

I think sometimes of the English professor I might have become, accepting one minor appointment after another, moving from college town to college town across the American landscape, each time erecting my tent anew. My tent would have been Blake, Wordsworth, and Joyce; George Eliot and Virginia Woolf. I could never quite picture myself enduring it. Also, I could not picture succeeding. Me: the singular sensation in a pool of two hundred and two applicants who lands the one precious job. Me? I have too many questions about Kierkegaard. I have too many questions about how toilets and furnaces work. I wanted one place to live in and one job to do. I wanted Yasnaya Polyana.

My early ideas of nomad life came not only from the Sioux but also from the desert. The sources are obscure, probably multiple—TV and movies, books, especially the Bible, as illustrated in story and coloring books. The biblical lands were hot, sandy places where grown men wore sandals and robes instead of pants. The men could not farm the land but instead herded sheep on foot. (Full masculinity did not arrive in human history until my country brought forth cowboys.) Water was precious. It had to be gotten from wells instead of faucets. No one other than the king seemed to have much of a house.

Like my ideas about Indians, my desert imaginings belonged to a collective American fantasy. I incorporated whatever my surroundings tossed up in a process exactly opposite to the Arnoldian quest laid out for me much later in college. As a child, I was not in the business of seeking out the best or deliberately refining my taste. Pure gratification pulled me along.

The Araby of my childhood had no analogue in the actual world. It came in a faux-desert kit that included dense blue sky, white sand, and stallions caparisoned in red and gold. In bedtime reveries, especially in summer, I sometimes found myself crawling across a burning wasteland. I was battered and wounded, dying of thirst. Just when all hope seemed lost, I came upon an oasis. I was ministered to inside a tent where everything was very clean. The tent was hung with bolts of silk and thick with beautiful pillows. Miraculously, there were no bugs.

It turned out I was a spy. I was Ilya Kuryakin, the handsome sidekick on *The Man from U.N.C.L.E.* Somehow I had wandered into a scene from *Ben Hur*. In *Ben Hur* the horses were everything. They came in matched sets of four and trained for the chariot races. A white quartet entered my tent, four housebroken steeds. Someone fed them sugar cubes, which they scooped up in a single motion of velvet lips. (I had sneaked sugar cubes from the cupboard in our church kitchen, from the drawer at the Masonic hall when Mom was there to set up for Eastern Star; a kind of horse host, they dissolved on my reverent tongue.)

My desert was the outdoors as it should be and as I knew it not to be. When hot weather came to Plainville, it brought moist suffocating nights of pestering mosquitoes. Dust, hot wind, and needle-dry grass composed the daytime hours. In my desert oasis, though, a caressing breeze blew. It was unaccountably mild. Purple night was falling. *Lie back on these clean sheets, these cool, tassled pillows.*

Such were my reveries as the fans droned, and I, like every person in town, shifted ceaselessly on the sheets, trying to find an overlooked cool spot as I covered my head against the dentist-drill song of a mosquito diving for my ear. I would slap myself in the darkness, lie seething and alert. Why on earth were poets so full of the praises of summer? They had to be talking about some other place.

The train would pass through then, burrowing deep into my discomfort, sounding its sustained saxophone note as it headed to bigger places. I would thrill with the sense of everything coming.

I might be borne out of this town, might land somewhere pristine and bugless. I might be rich, brilliant, famous. Only not-yet, not-yet, not-yet. That was the song of the train speeding off. I did not have to leave home just yet.

Almost five years after we moved to Eastboro, I was assigned to accompany a group of journalists going to Israel. Most journalists spend years longing to be sent somewhere, anywhere, at company expense. But I did not want to go. The trip was scheduled for June, when our roses and peonies bloom. Also, my birthday is in June, as is my husband's and our wedding anniversary. In my view, June was no time to leave home.

In South Dakota, June breezed through our house with a light touch. It had a mournful, valedictory feel. June was the start of summer, the official child's paradise. Yet it was also the end of school—the end of order and self-testing, the two poles from which my identity seemed suspended. I had no use for paradise. I was Persephone's photo negative, descending into darkness as spring advanced, dying as the earth came alive.

Yet I was excited about my birthday. Guided by whatever notions guided mothers in those days, Mom delivered magical parties featuring games and favors, cake and ice cream. She would fuss over fruit cups, making a saw-toothed container of an orange, cutting it just so as Grandma observed: "The kids won't even notice that."

But I did notice. The cake decked with tiny American flags in honor of Flag Day, the color-coordinated napkins and punch fizzing with ginger ale, balloons and streamers in a color scheme— all of these things telegraphed a sense of occasion. A birthday lifted time outside its ordinary bounds and reinforced the notion "You are special." At the same time, birthdays were deeply democratic. Every kid I knew got a turn at being the special one. And perhaps because of the flags, I connected birthdays with being an American and therefore with all American triumphs, especially the ones depicted in war movies. We were the Americans, the good guys—a special people sitting on top of the world, honored with cupcakes and candles from our very earliest days. Birthdays were part of the secret formula of our success.

My birthday in Israel felt like a non-birthday—a day to do what was professionally required. On that day our group waited for what seemed like an hour in the cramped vestibule of the U.S. embassy in Tel Aviv, finally passing one by one through a metal detector. We were relieved of our cameras and blue tote bags and ushered to a featureless conference room with a dropped ceiling and over-powerful air conditioner. As I hugged my knees trying to keep warm, the droning ambassador told us precisely nothing. (The Clinton administration favored advancing the peace process.) Then, after saying nothing for fifteen minutes, he apologized but said he had to go to Jerusalem.

I looked at him with new interest.

Jerusalem.

I was sitting across a bare table from a man who said he had to go to Jerusalem. He said it as easily as someone in Providence might say he was going to Boston, as my parents might say they were driving over to Ortonville or Twin Brooks. *I have to go to Jerusalem.*

The ambassador left; his assistant juggled rhetorical balls for us for another half hour. Then we filed out again into the bright sun of Tel Aviv. We threaded our way through the cement gumdrops meant to thwart trucks bearing explosives expressly for the embassy, a special package just for Americans. *Happy birthday!*

I squinted at Tel Aviv. This was the land of the Bible—the land

I had colored in coloring books. And there was no resemblance. Tel Aviv was a modern instance of the anti-pastoral. Blocky apartment buildings on cement stilts lined the streets. The main gesture toward beautification was the rows of annuals planted in highway median strips, irrigation pipes running alongside them like train tracks in the sandy soil. Likewise the hotels, though modern and comfortable, were something less than beautiful. Yet the crescent of Mediterranean beaches over which they stood watch elevated them. A broad garland of sand met the aquamarine water and invited long dreamy walks. Imagine: A tribe wanders for centuries, endures all the horrors of exile and oppression, and its reward, finally, is a resort. In Tel Aviv the Israelites posted their umbrellas in the sand and looked out at the blue horizon.

After our trip to the embassy, we scattered to dine in the shorefront cafés. A half-dozen of us met up again after nightfall to stand, pant legs rolled, knee-deep in the water. The evening was mild and pleasant, bugless. We looked up at the stars. A passing jet was bringing another group to the homeland. Most of us were not Jewish and so did not regard this brave, modern city, assembled in mere decades as intimate geography. Yet it was impossible to be there and not think of the homeland idea. Excitement, even bliss, crossed the sky in the form of that plane. In just this way, we ourselves had entered the country scarcely forty-eight hours before. We all began to speak of home, of the people we loved and had just left. Did they know that at this moment we stood in the Mediterranean peering at stars, tracking one jet, a temporary community, and thinking of them?

Behind us was a broad well-lit promenade where young people strolled. Music played in a café near the water. It was hard to conceive of missiles falling on this city, but they had, only a few years earlier, during the Gulf War. Deeper into the city, on a concrete plain that might have been imported from New York, Yitzhak Rabin had been shot. It was not a Palestinian after all who did it, who so violently objected to the prime minister's effort to make peace. It was a Jew. Some Israelis said it was a good thing. Schoolgirls wrote love letters to Rabin's jailed assassin. The country was thick with unsettled arguments.

"Does this place feel tense to you?" Eric said into the quiet. He was a radio host from Milwaukee, tall, witty, and black, an unusual presence in Tel Aviv. We all knew what he meant. Things were fine and not fine. Ehud Barak had just been elected prime minister, with vows to wrap up a peace deal before you could say millennium. The congenitally guarded Israelis were punchy with hope. We took deep breaths of the lovely disputed air before heading back to our rooms.

There were eight of us. We made a home for ourselves on the tour bus, became a little tribe. Crossing the hot, dry land, we established origins and family histories, college ties, and career paths. We were from Florida and Texas, from Seattle and Atlanta and cities in Ohio. We drank bottle after bottle of the water kept in a special compartment for us. We took notes, worked to understand where we were—why it was so intensely fought over; how such a barren place could be perceived as the promised land, the only place in all creation that would do. And we each felt mystically connected to our guide, Menachem, a grizzled witness to a good chunk of Israel's modern history. Witness, and actor: There are few mere bystanders in the Middle East. As a boy, Menachem would sometimes be wakened in the night so that a Jew being smuggled into the country might use his bed for a few hours.

Later, like most Israelis, he became a soldier. Their arms, after World War II, were purchased in Eastern Europe. The first rifle he was handed had Nazi insignia on it.

Menachem told of how, when he was young, he hated the Jews of Europe for going meekly to the gas chambers. Now when he thought of his hatred, he trembled with shame. He told us this at Yad Vashem, the Holocaust memorial overlooking Jerusalem, where a tape continuously tells the names of all the children who died, taking three years to pronounce them and then beginning again.

He led us to the Sea of Galilee, set among green hills ascending to the Golan. The sea was a cold blue, surprisingly big, with little around it beyond fields of banana and avocado trees. A sign with an arrow said CAMPING. Out on the water, windsurfers were taking advantage of the stiff breeze. Storms came up suddenly on the Galilee, Menachem said. You had to be ready.

He showed us the rocky remains of the synagogue in Capernaum where it is believed Jesus first taught, amazing his audience. We drove up the hill associated with the Sermon on the Mount. At the top is a church (the Christians being unable to let things be). It is skirted by immaculate swaths of green and enjoys a fine view of the Galilee. Menachem insisted that we read the famous words of the sermon aloud. Someone produced a Bible, and the beatitudes rolled from our skeptical journalists' lips.

These were the stomping grounds of the big cheese of my childhood. And yet it was all so tentative. Every site was "believed to be" or "by tradition." Outside Bethlehem, Menachem pointed to two separate fields where shepherds supposedly saw the Star of the East—a matter, like much else in Israel, of dispute. How to connect with Bethlehem when many scholars now believe Jesus was born in Nazareth?

From Galilee, after stops related to kibbutz life, military life, and Israeli security, we would at last turn toward Jerusalem, the ultimate city of metaphor, just as Jesus finally had. We would follow the path the ambassador had mentioned so casually.

Jerusalem is not so many miles from Capernaum. But it would have seemed far to one on foot, especially in the heat of June. The heat in Capernaum was as heavy as wool, the most overpowering that I have ever felt. It drained us of intention, even of words. We wanted only to sit immobile under the trees. We were like the skinny cats that lay among the ruins, that would not have troubled themselves if ten thousand mice had scampered by. I could not imagine wanting to do a thing in such heat; I felt like a child visiting Regine. What idea would seem so urgent it would move you even to speak where you sat, let alone address a crowd? What idea would compel you to walk to the next village, never mind Jerusalem?

In Jesus' day Jerusalem was the big time. Going to Jerusalem was the equivalent of a young American's setting out to make it in New York. By the time we finally got there, we had been on the road for most of the day. As our bus climbed into the city, past imposing churches and tiers of pale limestone buildings, anxiety gripped me. I felt faintly the overlay of my journey to college, the same stomach-seizing dread that comes with some idea of the hard thing you must do. Jesus' legendary triumphal entry into the city of course turned disastrous overnight. Jerusalem did not work out for him at all.

Menachem pointed to a low green place, the Garden of Gethsemane, and later to a still deeper valley where, he said, the Canaanites for many years had sacrificed their first-born to Moloch. I did not remember that valley being in the coloring books. I had not heard of any child killings. Abraham, after all, forebore.

We were silent, peering out, absorbing Jerusalem, the deep taproot of America. I forgot about home and the June roses. I felt alert. Fear and ecstasy had ranged together here for centuries, and Jerusalem seemed, on first sight, both familiar and inevitable. I felt that Grandma Andersen was with me: I searched the city's contours on her behalf but also for myself. I suppose, like everyone who comes to Jerusalem, I was looking for something, even hoping, weakly, absurdly, for a revelation. Certainly it happens. Menachem told us about "Jerusalem syndrome." People arrive in the city and become unhinged, thinking they are Mary or Jesus or that they know the day when Armageddon will arrive. The city medical establishment is specially equipped to deal with them.

But I remained quite rational. We checked into our hotel, went separately to our rooms, and showered off what felt like several days' grime. The Laromme was the kind of luxury place that you might pick for a splurge weekend, maybe for a birthday ending in a zero. The rooms had mini-bars and two phones and firm mattresses, thick carpeting, marble baths. One morning, on TV, I watched Fred Astaire dancing his heart out above a line of Hebrew subtitles.

My room had a modest balcony. I could stand on it and observe a slice of Jerusalem's backyard, which I did over and over again. I turned off the temperature-controlled air, went onto the balcony, and studied the honey-colored light. I told myself this was Jerusalem and that I would not be back, so look, look. And still I was stunned, disbelieving, as I labored to make it stick.

• • •

Jerusalem is sand-colored. The hills are spiked with black-green trees shaped like popsicles. At the heart of Jerusalem is the Old City, divided into quarters as in some symbolic vision. Its narrow passageways wind past stalls selling spices, necklaces, pottery, postcards, and creche sets carved from olive wood. Without Menachem, it would have been easy to get lost. With him, I could indulge my prairie soul's craving for nooks.

At the edge of the Old City, on the high ground the Jews call the Temple Mount, Muslim officials guarded the Dome of the Rock and the Al-Aqsa Mosque. They glared as they admitted us, shoeless, with shoulders and knees properly covered. *(This is bound to be lost on you, decadent Western infidel. And by the way, Jerusalem belongs to us. Write your congressman.)* Below the Temple Mount at the Western Wall, Jews prayed, just as fervently regarding Jerusalem as their capital. To them, the mount is the site of the ancient temple, twice destroyed except for the single remaining wall.

The Muslims built their eye-popping gold-domed house of worship right on the same spot, hundreds of years later. This, they said, was where Muhammad, their great religious leader, ascended to heaven. This, the Jews say, on a rock right within the mosque, is the place where God tested their great ancestor Abraham, with the request that he sacrifice his son. Two stories, two voices, one conclusion: *This is the place.* From inside, I gazed up at the dome, grew dizzy from the florid Arabic script so strange and beautiful-looking, words as decoration because of the Muslim suspicion of images. Here was a great mosaic of assertion, punctuated by brilliant blues and reds.

Jerusalem's Church of the Holy Sepulchre, which occupies Golgotha and the reputed site of Christ's tomb, likewise has a no-shoulders and no-knees rule. It too is contested ground. The day we visited it was thick with pilgrims, clergy, and the merely curious. Bands of monks were working their way through the stations of the cross, in the one place on Earth where they can be asserted to be literal. (Here, Christ was condemned to death; here, he fell in the street.)

Stewardship of the building is divided among Christian sects—Roman Catholic, Armenian, Greek Orthodox, Coptic, Syrian—and each clings fiercely to its piece. Here was the self-proclaimed home of the true Christian's heart. Yet the Church of the Holy Sepulchre was notably without peace, choking with incense and clamorous with chants, crowded in every corner with people who had come in search of the world's absolute center. A stern-looking priest shooed us away from the "tomb"—a mausoleum-like structure within a great hall—so that robed men could line up there and conduct their devotions. Elsewhere inside the structure, a long line of people waited to stick a hand beneath an altar and feel the hole said to have held the cross on which Jesus died.

I thought not of God but of churches, of the strenuous, soul-shredding arguments of theologians. I felt the weight of doctrines tediously laid out over the centuries, of the endless arguments about what was true, who was right. I was not offended exactly; only I did not feel that God was there, in that place. It did not seem surprising either. Always, I had pictured a barren hill.

The words that confound every Christian and structure the celebration of spring came to me: "He is not here." Christianity is built around absence—the absence of Jesus and the promise of his return. You might therefore expect Christians in Jerusalem to stand back, give way. But they make their claim just like everybody else. The Old City is still marked off by walls built during the Crusades. *Here,* the walls insist. *One God. One truth. Our truth in this place.* Those who disagreed were relieved of their lives and crammed onto the Happy Day Express.

Our house in Eastboro was built in or close to 1896. It was the year Theodor Herzl published *The Jewish State,* the famous manifesto outlining his vision of a Jewish homeland. The Jewish dream of the tribe may be the most thorough, the most thwarted and longstanding, in all of human history. As such it seems at times to stand for all others, even the Palestinians'. The irony grows increasingly tormenting, is lost on fewer and fewer people.

So long as it is connected to place, and it invariably is, the dream of the tribe has something deeply impossible at its heart. I reluctantly faced this in Denmark. Yet one Friday evening in the Laromme, I was overwhelmed by the sight of a large group of people—an extended family, I supposed—who had gathered in a banquet room. The solemnity of the sabbath dinner was over, and now they were singing and clapping, dancing. A collective joy I had never experienced spilled from that room. The unseen ballast of the Holocaust only seemed to make the celebrants soar higher. *We are still here!* Who could deny them this miracle, a miracle of connection? I watched with awe and longing. Was this, after all, what I was seeking—this, more than the lonely approach on bare feet to God?

The next evening we were to leave. But first we shared an astonishingly good dinner at a Moroccan restaurant. We sat at a large round table in dim, dreamy lighting. All the dishes were meant to be shared. Centuries of experience with food and seasoning seemed to have culminated for our benefit. We ate with wonder, urging one another to try this, try that. I thought of the typical fare at U.S. restaurants, the personal allotment of something fried with cheese melted over it. Soon we would disperse to our separate TGI Fridays. At the end of our meal, a waiter poured mint tea into tiny cups from several feet high above them and did not lose a drop. Home seemed an abstraction; I did not want to leave Menachem or this place where the place meant so much to its people.

After a long interval of half-sleep, a night that seemed to last two nights, we landed at Kennedy Airport. Our journalists' group dissolved. So did the planeload of mostly Jewish people with whom we had shared the sky. Many of the men wore yarmulkes or the dark garb of the Orthodox. They suddenly seemed all that was left of Israel, and I felt a mild panic as they melted into the mass of traveling Americans. Every day a little diaspora.

A bus took me to my departure terminal, where I saw almost exclusively the casually dressed people of my heterodox nation, a highly mobile people for whom the idea of a homeland was not an issue. Brisk, practical Americans: Their multiple ideas of religion were portable, not tied to sacred sites. We had met such people among the Israelis and also among the Palestinians—the practical ones willing to accept a divided land and get on with it, to carry religion lightly. But the Palestinian leaders, the men of Fatah, stood us up. At the appointed hour, we were served tea by a gracious assistant and left alone with a portrait of Yasser Arafat. For him, religion never was the point. It was something like an alternate fuel source. Conflated with a passion for home, it would burn as fiercely as you pleased. What else did he need to know? Arafat, too, was a practical man.

When I got back to Eastboro, the place looked unnaturally green, as though a wild fit of irrigation had gone on while I was away. A small depression hit me, reprising the summer mourning of my childhood. For a span of time that resisted measurement, the journalists' group had been my community; so, oddly, had been the people of Israel, for whom place is as vital as water. For them, being-in-the-land is a component of consciousness in a way it is not for Americans. I felt the world lose intensity, felt it relax into mere commerce.

I thought of a man I met once in Cambridge at a small party. I was in my mid-thirties and had come looking for something. The man was older, articulate, a bearded somebody threatening to become a wisdom figure as he held forth to the group. He had embraced and discarded various systems of religious thought, he explained, had even been a minister at one point. And now, after years of searching, he had achieved the final, perfect result of his quest: "I have faith but no belief."

Six words, they came to me repeatedly over the next several days: *I have faith but no belief.* Belief was what divided people, made one group inevitably assert its superiority over another, even claim the very ground. Any thinking person could see that. In six words the man at the party had defined the place where I unwillingly stood, and had stood for years. They were brave words, I felt, but sad ones too. No one who carried them in her heart was bound to find much in Jerusalem.

Tolstoy, busy late in life constructing his own Jerusalem (Christ's kingdom in Russia), would have found the Cambridge man's position intolerable. In fact, left alone with him, Tolstoy probably would have wiped the floor with this guy. It is preposterous enough to be certain of one's uncertainty, he might have said. But Tolstoy's main objection, I suspect, would simply have been this: The man had stopped looking. He had closed the books. After that, what remained to be done? We see Anna's dainty foot on the station platform; we see her push off. Tolstoy could not abide it. He had to conclude with Lenin.

There is the cradle of civilization and then our own. We draw in strands made up of our parents and idle summers, friends and romances, school projects and first jobs. The place where it all began has a strange hypnotic pull. And yet Americans do not expend much passion over place. Occasionally someone will sit in a redwood tree, but it is the tree she wants to save, not a sacred grove where shared mysteries have transpired. We are expected and expect ourselves to get up and move, to assume our stations tending the great economic engine that is the United States. Large numbers of us inhabit the world provisionally, feel like perpetual guests in our own land. Americans change residences, on average, every six years.

Even so, in our everyday exile we may get moments of extreme orientation. One day the train goes by. I see it from my study window and think of nothing special. But on another day I see the trees laid low as the cars rattle past. I see the Western Wall of the temple, where men wearing black bob in prayer, their courtship of God so avid that the rest of life is only time in between. And then even the remains of the temple fall. The sky opens like a garish bloom, stretching high and wide. Behold: There is nothing but prairie.

THE SHORE OF LAKE MICHIGAN

I WAS at first overwhelmed by the library, a modern structure, golden it seemed, overlooking the lake. But shortly, I began to love its air-conditioned, glassed-in elegance, its silence, its cool plenty verging on excess. I was seventeen, still in high school, attending Northwestern University's summer institute for debaters.

Mom had been here years before me, closing the impossible gap between our prairie farmlands and the city of Chicago, crossing several states to reach Illinois, in a more unlikely bid for the world than even mine was. Sorting through the Sixth Street attic years later, we found papers showing that her group had included Charles Kuralt. In adulthood he became the well-known TV journalist, popular for wistful on-the-road tales of hidden America. Then, when he died, we all found out he had a hidden life of his own, a second life complete with longstanding mistress and a house far away from it all in Montana.

Nights at the institute were devoted to library research. We split the material we found into fragments, then bound the pieces to index cards. There were special rooms set aside just for typing. I carried my heavy portable Olympia with me like a bag of groceries, hugging it to my chest. I teetered on my clogs. I wore shorts and a T-shirt and a bandanna scarf on my head to hold my hair back while I worked. My hair was long and fine, and every day I glanced at the boys. But I was consecrated to research: I loved the idea of it and even the word itself, its good-faith optimism, its long unwinding promise of order and ultimately of understanding. The surfeit of materials pleased me the way a thundering herd once had.

At the time, it seemed that my main discovery was that you could not do serious research in Plainville. In Northwestern's library I checked the reference area, the never-ending card catalogue, the capacious zone—so fresh with new wood, so cunningly organized—we importantly called government docs. Every element dwarfed its counterpart in Plainville and sang, finally, not of itself but of the question *What is Plainville like?*

Every night I was in the library; all of us were, keeping an eye on one another, competing always, wondering who had found the killer quote that would finish off an opponent. More than that, we were practicing for the competition college would bring. When it was time to quit, I would walk briskly back to the dorm on a path that wound through pine trees. It was a heart-pounding trip, an interval of praying that no one would leap on me in the dark. This was not Plainville with its unlocked doors.

I felt better each time I made it safely back, better the more evidence I accumulated on whether elementary and secondary schools should be exclusively financed by the federal government. (All our copies of *Crisis in the Classroom* by Charles Silberman were well thumbed and full of underlinings.) I might just make it through three weeks away from home.

The counselors and faculty came from prestigious colleges.

Nearly all were men and most were adored. They were brilliant, witty, and theatrical. Most important, they took us utterly seriously. Each morning we gathered in an auditorium where the institute director addressed us. He had a thick black beard and wore a neatly pressed short-sleeved shirt. On cloudy days he carried a full-length black umbrella. He never moved or spoke with haste, and he entranced us with the sense that, whatever else might be going on in the nation that day, it could not possibly be as important as what was going on here. We were learning, he said, "the art of advocacy." He said it as though it were a calling, the work of saints. It was so exalted, in fact, that it was granted this magisterial setting on the shore of Lake Michigan: Everyone could see that. We dug in, sensing some profound reward across the water. We were shiny with faith.

On a June day nine years later, my family gathered in the same place. It was morning, hazy and overcast, the day of Charlie's graduation from the business school, and we had time for a stroll along the lake. We were in our best clothes. Mom had on a dark blue dress and heels. I do not know how long we had been walking or how far we had gone when one of her legs began to drag. Her leg looked like rubber, a dummy's leg. I had been living in Providence. I had never seen this before.

Mom laughed. She said: "This darn leg."

She was just tired. She would be okay, she said, if she rested for a few minutes. We got her to the car. She sat in the driver's seat, her legs facing out, touching the ground, while she waited to be normal again.

Charlie and Dad and I stood looking at the lake. Nobody said much. We all knew what it was.

. . .

When the granddaughter of Niels Ebbesen Hansen started to get sick, I was a child. The Sees had completed a short move just a few houses down the block to one almost directly across from ours. It was a grand house by Plainville standards, with solemn, dark-stained woodwork everywhere. I envied the kids' having a real fire-place to hang their Christmas stockings on; every year Charlie and I propped ours up on chairs.

Upstairs in the Sees' house were three bedrooms and a bath-room. Downstairs was a dining room with a small room adjoining it, for the piano or sewing or whatever extra thing you needed to do. Off the living room was a sunporch. The kitchen was big enough (though barely) for all six of the Sees to eat in, and for the big two-way radio used to reach Mr. See when he was going from farm to farm, looking after cows. Mrs. See could call on it and find out where he was going next or when he was coming home for supper.

I knew the Sees' house intimately. I knew which cabinet con-tained the packages of cookies, if there were any, and where the potato chips were kept. I knew the kitchen wall clock was set five minutes ahead to ensure that everyone made it to school on time. I knew that in the fall, brown bags full of apples would be kept cool in the side-door entrance, called the basement-way, where coats and scarves hung crowded together on pegs.

Mrs. See was den mother to Charlie's Cub Scout pack and ran the boys' meetings in the kitchen. Once she showed them how to melt old 45 records so that two sides could be curled up like a po-tato chip, and then you had an ashtray. The boys wore dark blue shirts to their meetings and bright golden neckerchiefs. They did a two-finger salute and vowed to obey the laws of the pack.

The whole family loved that house, Mrs. See especially. But she was having problems. In Plainville the doctors did not know what was wrong with her. She went to an out-of-town doctor next. Because the problem was not in my house, and I was in a world of horses, I did not know about a diagnosis or a prognosis or anything else.

Then one day Mrs. See got a cane, and it looked funny on a mother instead of on an old man. We got used to seeing her with a cane, and then it seemed it was no time at all before her bed was moved downstairs into the room that was for something extra. She quit going upstairs and had to trust that it was in order, that the kids were keeping it clean.

The Sees hired Mrs. Wipf, a white-haired woman in an apron and heavy shoes, who came over and vacuumed and dusted. I can remember her on the stairs, polishing the woodwork canyons where Maryann and I sometimes played with our horses. Her movements were awkward and slow yet sufficient to carry her to the second floor.

Each time I visited I turned hot with a child's sense of injustice. Imagine not being able to go upstairs in your own house: not once. These were the days, the weeks, the months when we were all getting used to seeing the wheelchair and pretending it was no more remarkable than an end table. *What news from upstairs?* For Mrs. See it was a lost kingdom, a former homeland fondly recalled. The master bedroom now belonged to Meg, the oldest daughter. Mrs. See was in exile in her own house.

She did not mention it. Ordinary household disputes went on every day, and from her wheelchair she was the referee. Whose turn was it to unload the dishwasher? Who had not put in the required half hour of practice time on the piano? Shouldn't Mark be out the door by now, beginning his paper route? The topic was never multiple sclerosis—never MS, the shorthand among those who know.

Meg talked about it when we were walking places. Plainville kids were almost always on the hoof. Because the town was small, there was no technical need for us to be driven most places. Meg was good at thinking about life and its deep meaning and had a lot to say about it. I liked listening to her.

"My mom says that right now is your heaven or your hell," she said. It seemed wise and true, a sweeping challenge to the standard views of the afterlife we had picked up in church or on religious TV shows. I guessed that it meant it was up to you to do something about it if you felt sad. But I did wonder about God, and sensed there was something open and unknown about him. The God I heard of in church was all love. Jesus assured us this was so. But why did he let this bad thing happen to Mrs. See?

Meg and I walked over every inch of that town in every season, discussing and debating as we sold Girl Scout cookies or poppies for the veterans. (When we sold Girl Scout nuts, elderly ladies came to the door and announced, "I can't have nuts," as if they had been waiting their whole lives to tell the world.) As we walked, our snowboots made a plastic scraping sound. In summer our tennis shoes hit the sidewalk with soft quick slaps, and sometimes we were careful to skip the cracks and other times we paid no attention.

Eventually we wore good shoes with heels, and nylons. We picked our way carefully along ice-crusted walks to the high school, too proud to put on anything sturdy, and impatient with the idea of carrying our shoes in a shoe bag. Our skirts were as short as we dared, and when we passed through the school's double doors, the sudden blast of heat flushed our knees red. Our heels clicked on the linoleum floors, which the janitors kept spotless. The halls smelled faintly of cleaning compound and polish.

When the Sees left Sixth Street for their custom-made house at the edge of town, I was in junior high. It seemed that this, finally, was where they would stay. But when Meg and I graduated from high school, the family moved again, and then again, to a series of smaller spaces in larger towns. The two younger girls learned everything there was to know about keeping house condominium-style, including storage solutions. The Sixth Street house must have seemed to all of them like some genteel estate from which they had been expelled years ago, back when they were the Romanovs.

Nerves are coated with a substance called myelin, which helps one nerve transmit information to another. When I think of myelin, I picture the pink goo they smear on you when they want to measure the electrical activity of your heart with an EKG. In MS, the goo breaks down. It is as though the body itself is trying to get rid of the goo. One nerve cannot talk to the next. "Take up your pallet and walk." The message starts in the brain, slides off the rails, does not get through. Foot and brain might as well belong to two different people. The distance between foot and brain has become infinite.

With Mom there was one early sign. She was playing the organ at church, and her eyes were bothering her. Something strange was happening to her vision. One eye went blank. She went to an out-of-town doctor to have it checked. The doctor could not come up with anything, and then it went away. For years there was nothing more.

I remember feeling cross about it, in the selfish way of a child. The way things were arranged in my world required Mom to be up and running, not a problem. I did not want a mom whose problems were the center of life. I had a lot to think about without that. Besides, Mom did not have time to be sick. She had to get the paper out, had to be at choir and Job's Daughters and Eastern Star and Church Circle and study club and the City Council meeting. It was Dad who was the one who got everything— migraines and back problems and colds; he was laid low by every bug that came through town. Mom set her mouth in a line and kept going.

Knowing what she was beginning to know, Mrs. See had her thoughts about Mom's eye problem but was reluctant to speak. And then she could only shrug as the years went on and Mom was still okay. Who knew with this darned disease?

Was multiple sclerosis hereditary? Could you get it by crossing the street to have coffee with your neighbor and maybe drinking accidentally from her cup? Or was the main criterion simply that you had to be a mother in a particular South Dakota town on the street called Sixth during a brief golden age that history somehow missed?

What pernicious bacterium wafted down our wholesome avenue on what breeze? What virus shot into my mother's bloodstream when her hand brushed what countertop, hauled which garbage? What malevolent chemical action was set in motion when she crossed our pesticide-rich fields to look at a 4-H animal or a barn hit by lightning? What business of cells turns an immune system on itself so that it reaches out and destroys every impulse toward life? Was it a mosquito that bit Meg's mother, and mine? Was it something carried by our egregious yappy little dogs, Chihuahuas in full or in part? Was it our air, our water, our own dear native soil, the potential of which Grandpa Hansen had seen, and to which he had given his whole heart?

Was it our fault?

Vain, demanding children, consumed with our own futures, how we would dazzle, what we would be, in love with our own stories—had we tired our mothers so much that illness found its way in? The subway doors open and close, open and close on me, on Meg, and we ride the Red Line, the Green Line, and we are running away just as much as we are running toward.

It has been forty years since Mrs. See first noticed her legs beginning to falter, and still nobody knows what multiple sclerosis really is or what causes it. For a long time, doctors diagnosed it by ruling out everything else. They would tell the new patients about the cases where people get brief spells, and then it is over—spells and then they would lead active lives for many years. Vision problems, balance problems, trouble walking, etc. etc., would come and go. This kind—relapsing-remitting, it was called—in fact appears to characterize the majority of cases. But where were these mild cases? Everywhere, it seemed, but on Sixth Street.

"Hi, folksies," Mom used to say when she was feeling good. I can still picture her in her stylish short dresses, her tall "these-boots-are-made-for-walking" boots, a fashion statement that did double duty in our drastic winters. Mom forded the drifts in knee-high red or brown or white patent leather. She trotted down to the courthouse for the week's proceedings, stopped at Rasmussen Drug to get the right color candles for a holiday display at home, dropped off an ad to be shared with the *Sun*.

"Hi, folksies! What's new?"

Mom finally did get a diagnosis, about two years after that day we were all together in Evanston. By then it was almost an after-thought. Mom was fifty. Dad ran the numbers through his head, plotting the arc to retirement as he wondered how long she could keep going. One thing they knew: She would not be receiving disability payments. Under the way the *Herald Advance* was organized, they were required to send in payroll taxes only on one of them, and they had picked Dad. As far as the U.S. government knew, Mrs. Round-the-Clock had been home watching *Days of Our Lives* all those years. My parents had picked out Dad for calamity and they had picked wrong.

I knew Dad was lying awake nights wondering what to do. Who would buy a weekly in a dinky two-weekly town? Only a crazy person.

I called Charlie. "Should I go home? Should I try to help out for a few years?"

"No. That's a no-brainer." He did not explain, and he did not really need to. I thought of us walking around the table, gathering masonic books, so mote it be. Dad, when I asked, also said no.

On the other hand, it was not as though I had any great career going. A week after Charlie's graduation from business school, I had begun a new job as a reporter for *The Providence Journal.* I was not exactly tearing up the place, even now that I had some idea of what I was doing. But the pay was better than at the *Herald Advance.* And most days, when you finished writing your story, you could go home.

Which is what I did. In my one-bedroom in Providence, I slept the sleep of a dead person, falling into oblivion even as I knew Dad was lying awake sorting through the impossibilities again and again. Mom had a cane and tried to hide it from view when she was not using it. The cane embarrassed her.

I was embarrassed too, but for reasons all my own. I was in jour-
nalism, the exact field I had left Plainville to avoid. What was I
proving by not going home? I did not have children enrolled in superior schools and soaking up the cultural advantages of the East.
I did not even have a husband. I did not even have a boyfriend.

The conventional advice for MS patients is to rest so that the disease does not get any worse than it has to. Mom tried to figure out
how to cut back but had no better idea now than in the days when
she wanted to sneak off and reline the kitchen cupboards with con-
tact paper. Friends started coming by the office on press day and
helping out, saying they had nothing else to do. A wheelchair arrived, but Mom hated it even more than the cane and insisted on
sitting in a real chair at the dinner table.

They sold the little house they had redone, with its cozy upstairs, the house Mom had made so charming with her do-it-
yourself projects. (Was it the paint stripper that had gone to work
on her myelin?) They moved into a condo on the edge of town. It
was modern, all on one level with wide passages perfect for wheel-
chairs and a view of the truck transfer station out back. Then—
and this is the only place where the plot of my family history goes
halfway right—a crazy person came to town.

Bert Tollefson reminded me of something I read once, which is
that there are only two great plots in literature: One is a stranger
comes to town, and I forget the other. Bert Tollefson was as nice a
young man as anyone would want to meet. He was working at a
weekly about a hundred miles away and had reached the point
where he thought it would be nice to be on his own.

We were all dumbstruck as he arranged the financing and went
ahead. Mom and Dad would be able to disengage slowly. Mom

could keep writing for a while. Dad could stay on and advise, work in the back shop, until Bert had the hang of everything. Maybe the *Herald Advance* would be saved after all.

Bert Tollefson could be forgiven for imagining that our rival Victoria, now in her sixties, had some idea of the golden years that involved travel or puttering around the house. He did not understand that what he had arrived for was hand-to-hand combat and that you had to put everything you had into it, and more after that. You had to put in years of ancestral pride, have a sense that this was the only game on earth and it had your name on it.

Bert Tollefson struggled and began to sink. Victoria was not quitting. Far from it. She must have smelled triumph in the air.

"Don't come crying to me," Midwestern parents warn their children. Don't come crying to me if you spend your allowance all at once and there is nothing left over for a treat; when you fail to practice and then flub up in the recital; when we finally give you the exact bike you said you wanted or those bell-bottomed pants or the cotton candy, and then you say you would rather have had something else.

Mom does not come crying to me. She does not complain about not being able to walk, or to lift herself out of the wheelchair and onto the bed; about not being able to write a note or apply lipstick or brush the crumbs off herself with the one hand that still functions; about her bladder, which sometimes elects to perform at a moment she herself would not have picked.

She has gone off somewhere, become Job.

She reads. She is trying to learn French. She burrows deeper and deeper into Christian belief. Mostly she keeps that part to herself. But sometimes she mentions it, pressing me to return to church. Or she implies that illness has launched her on a spiritual pilgrimage. Once in a while regret surfaces: She feels guilty about something she did or did not do when Charlie and I were little.

Once, in the weekly letters she makes herself type one-handed to us, she tried to explain where she was with a Bible verse. She referred to Galatians 5:22-26. "But the fruit of the Spirit is love, joy, peace, longsuffering, gentleness, goodness, faith, meekness, temperance: against such there is no law. And they that are Christ's have crucified the flesh with the affections and lusts.

"If we live in the Spirit, let us also walk in the Spirit."

When I looked it up, the last line was all I could see.

Let us also walk. *Let us walk. Let us walk.*

After a few years, Bert Tollefson gave up. It was as though he had walked into the wrong movie, *Spartacus* instead of *How Green Was My Valley.* He went to a larger paper, a daily, where he could just write and not have all the headaches of being boss. This showed he was like me, which means he was exactly wrong for the job of saving the *Herald Advance.* He sold the paper to Mr. Engstrom, a businessman who owned a chain of small papers in Minnesota. Mr. Engstrom was a go-getter and he was a success. Maybe he had more gumption than Bert Tollefson. Our hopes lifted again.

Mr. Engstrom may have made the same wrong assumptions about Victoria that Bert did. He kept the paper going for a few more years, thinking surely she, a woman in her seventies, would be wrapping it up any minute now. Then Mr. Engstrom, who was not crazy but only a businessman, decided to cut his losses. He announced that because it was not profitable, the *Herald Advance* would be shutting down, and it did, after 112 years of publication.

. . .

I felt achy and sick the way you do when somebody dies. In retrospect, I could only see my parents as prizefighters, the stuff of legend.

Ding! Down goes Tollefson! Ding ding! And Engstrom, what a fighter, but still no match for the champion! How had my parents done it all those years? How had they held off loss, the yellow-toothed prospect that grinned at them every Monday? Then along came MS. *Ding! It's a knockout!*

With his iffy back, Dad began wearing a support-belt that attaches with Velcro so he could lift Mom. Luckily, Mom was not very big, but she started watching what she ate anyway so she would not be an ounce heavier than necessary. In restaurants I have seen her forgo lunch so she can have a special dessert: It really would be unbearable if you could not have dessert from time to time. A person needs something.

I think of my parents every day. But I think of Mom most when I am doing something physical: running; weeding; moving up and down the stairs of our house, up and down, as I fetch a load of laundry, haul the vacuum cleaner to the bedroom, carry down the wastebaskets for emptying; neaten up; rearrange; change sheets; try to make the place look orderly, balanced, beautiful. I scrub down the kitchen counter, put out vases of white cosmos from our garden, haul the boxes of Christmas ornaments up from the basement, and three weeks later neatly pack them up and haul them down again. My motion is full of fear and regret but also pleasure in the order of a home. The more I move, the more I am erased, gratefully expunged, in the housework that is my own perpetual memorial.

. . .

A picture from Charlie's graduation day shows him and Dad in ties and short-sleeved summer shirts, me in the jade green dress I bagged on sale at Bonwit Teller for my college roommate's wedding. Behind us, the lake is a soft gray-blue. You cannot see across. Mom, ignoring her darn leg, took the picture. It is Charlie's day. Right afterward, he will take a big step forward in life. As for me, in one week I will start my new job at the paper in Providence, the place where I will end up staying and staying.

In the picture we are all smiling while all I want to do is scream until the sound reaches the other side of the lake, circles the globe, fills the universe. I do not scream. I pretend that everything is fine. But my distress is out there for eternity now, dissolving time to the point where I can hear it perfectly well in childhood: I am a small girl in the Minneapolis train station, sleepy, my mind glittering with Christmas. I am waiting to go home; I am waiting for my life to begin. I cannot believe how good all this is.

YASNAYA POLYANA

ONE POSSIBILITY: An old man moves uncertainly along a train platform. He seems to be going somewhere, but where? Other passengers stream past him in both directions. The old man glances at them, recognizing no one. Suddenly he is stricken, collapses. Bystanders rush to his side and call for a doctor. They do not know that this is Tolstoy dying on the platform in a remote Russian town.

Another way of picturing the death of Tolstoy is to place him inside the station. We see him close up, the same bearded bewildered man. But we are conscious of a majestic structure, of the most beautiful light streaming in from high windows. It is the sad sweet light of benediction, a beam so perfectly round it looks as though it could be set upright and used to support a temple. This shaft of light makes us think of God, of angels moving up and down a ladder to heaven.

Because I do not have an image of the actual Astapovo Station in Russia, I am here picturing Grand Central Station in New York. It is familiar, our classic image of a great train station. Grand Central's many comings and goings make it a holy place, a repository of metaphor. In this particular image, the women passing by wear long dresses with cameos at their throats and elaborate hats. The men have pocket watches and starched collars. For now, these people have the stage. But soon we will need to consult pictures to know their kind. Suddenly, in their midst, Tolstoy clutches his chest and falls. Again people rush to the stranger's side. He says nothing, dies.

I have a third version, more private: Tolstoy sits on a wooden bench. It is long and curved to fit the seated human form. Lights shaped like marshmallows hang from the high ceiling. Porters move a few luggage carts across the floor, but for the most part the atmosphere is subdued. It is the Minneapolis depot in the dead of winter. It is night. Tolstoy appears healthy enough; he is merely an old man waiting. He looks at me and smiles. It is all just between him and me. Embarrassed, I look down at the floor, which is gritty from tracked-in snow and the passage of so many feet. I cannot bear Tolstoy's greatness. I cannot bear his messed-up life. I cannot bear having come so far only to find myself in this same place ever and forever, incapable of creating a single character other than myself.

Some years ago a group of sociologists proposed that to have modern consciousness is to have a homeless mind. It is a nifty theory, practically made for me. The sociologists were thinking especially about what went on in the heads of ordinary people leading ordinary lives. In every average schmo, they posited, the self is experienced in a partial and segmented way. It is borne about on a cloud of bureaucracy, experiences an unnatural split between its public and private versions, is bombarded by information, entrusts much to experts, dwells among strangers. Modern consciousness is urban consciousness: The house in Regine has disappeared.

This idea does not fit Tolstoy, mainly because he spent most of his years at Yasnaya Polyana. The man and the place were one. And then, one day, they were not. The sociologists cannot account for the case of Tolstoy, in exile from Yasnaya Polyana even as he moved through its handsome and familiar rooms, gazed at the familiar fields, and in spring watched the trees bud, tickling the sky with chartreuse.

In the end, the home Tolstoy proposed for humanity was a severe ethical universe that even he had trouble inhabiting. The odious Chertkov never tired of pointing out that the creature comforts of Yasnaya Polyana—which Tolstoy, under the thumb of the adamant Countess Sofya, continued to enjoy despite himself—were plainly not the thing for a true Tolstoyan. Fulfillment lay in renunciation.

The first time Tolstoy tried to leave, in 1884, he ended up coming back. Sofya was pregnant; a baby, her twelfth, was born. To make good his escape, Tolstoy had to try again. And of course, none of it happened in any of the ways I have imagined. The death of Tolstoy was a public occurrence, one we could even conveniently call the first modern media death. In other words, it was news—the thing to which I have been involuntarily bound my whole life. In the end, my idol left the country of art and crossed over into my own unremarkable terrain.

Tolstoy managed to sneak out of the house without waking his wife. But once he was on the train, he was soon recognized and even seemed to enjoy the commotion he caused. When he arrived at Astapovo Station in late October of 1910, he was not alone but with his doctor. Judged too ill to continue, he was brought inside the stationmaster's house—to die, as it happened.

Outside were swarms of reporters and photographers, even one movie camera. Tolstoy's wife and family came in on a special train car. Hordes of acolytes and admirers also appeared. For six days or so, everybody waited. The movie camera compressed it all, making a newsreel of the scene. The ever-dramatic Mrs. T. is on film pacing the platform.

At the time, most of the people who made a great to-do about Tolstoy's death barely remembered his novels. To them, he was the great critic of the Russian government, the great denouncer of religious orthodoxy. To later onlookers, he was the man who had tried truly to live as Christ taught and proved what a disastrous idea that is. Nearly everyone around him had suffered for it.

Tolstoy, too, suffered. For years, he had no peace either internally or in his outward life. In the end he feared that his wife planned to kill him. After he fled, he wrote to her: "Life is not a toy."

There is all the yearning of the universe in that sentence— "Life is not a toy." It drags every moment of human failure in its train. Why are we not wiser, happier, better? Why do we not make more of our chances?

"Search, always go on searching," Tolstoy said in his final delirium. How can we bear such an ending—its inconclusiveness, its weighty charge? How much easier to take is the ending attributed to Grandpa Andersen, the kind of finale that Tolstoy the writer, great creator of worlds, might have scripted for the redemption-minded Levin: "The ship is nearing the harbor, and Jesus, the pilot, is on board."

The last time I went home, it was winter. My husband and I crossed the blank terrain in a rental car. The horses in the fields were as woolly as bears. Their people were inside, making cookies, maybe, or wrapping. Except when we passed through towns, it seemed we had the prairie to ourselves; the swollen and expectant sky was ours too. Time slowed. We had all the time in the world. When night finally fell, we had trouble adjusting to the dark. Except in certain remote parts, the darkness of the East Coast is a peri-darkness: The place is lit up all the time. But on the prairie, darkness is still the darkness Ptolemy knew. It is deep, abiding, and private, and in it we are the spellbound center of everything.

A tiny town etched with Christmas lights emerged from the inky stillness: red, gold, blue, and green. It seemed improbable the lights should prevail against the extinguishing cold. The town's layout was the classic Midwestern kind: The main highway through was also the central commercial street. You are barreling along through open country, and then you must slow because suddenly it is a town. This one seemed silent, immersed in a deep pause. We glided alone past its handful of darkened stores, then were forced to halt as a freight train passed through. Boxcar followed boxcar in slow succession, the only sign of life, it seemed, for miles around. Because of the darkness, we felt more than saw their shapes.

As we waited, I thought of how this place was somebody's hometown. Left behind by who knew how many sons and daughters, it was the place they incessantly dreamed of. It was the place they would recognize in an instant, even if you shot them into space for a lap around the universe and the time they were away was measureless. We sat and watched the boxcars pass, as though they were a performance we had specifically come to attend. We were like the Hamms, knowing exactly where our end of the cosmic drama played out, pulling right up next to it in order to pay heed. I felt a tangy sensation at the back of my throat, acrid-oily but also sweet and breadlike. My nostrils filled. It was the smell of diesel fuel.

. . .

House. Yard. Fence. Already years have passed, and there are days when my new home seems so ordinary it is beyond notice. I turn on the radio, think of baking a pie, sort through the papers and throw out the ones we are done with. Volumes of Tolstoy sit idle on the shelf. The horses have quieted down. It seems a long time since I was the girl on fire to join the immortals. And why not a girl?, I said to myself fiercely back then. Nobody knew what I knew. I felt sure that any man who ever got a glimpse of my soul would die of surprise. The media would have to be called. *Doctors record first-ever death by surprise!* And the drop head: COLLEGE GIRL HARBORS OUTLANDISH AMBITION—WOULD BECOME TOLSTOY. Or something like that.

Where does such ambition go? Does the desire to create a world so easily collapse into the most everyday dreams imaginable? Instead of the vast teeming world, a small one bounded by pickets? Instead of Anna in her magnificent complexity, the perfect wallpaper? Or is the gathering power of one small life so strange and singular, the mystery of our being here so resplendent that it trumps everything—even the greatest art?

One thing I know. Whether I ever write another word or throw the whole business over for knitting, I will still harbor Tolstoy's warring sides: the one that loved the world; the one that could not bear its emptiness. Tolstoy the author could not find enough souls to inhabit. Tolstoy the sage wished only for God to inhabit him. How can the two ever be reconciled?

In buying a house, it would seem that I chose. I put my faith in things seen over things unseen. There is much to be said for a teacup, and I have said a fair amount of it here. What the stained-glass window told me, on the other hand, and what Tolstoy knew deep in his tired bones is that house and home are only ever accidentally the same.

A house is what it is: wood, nails, shingles. Ordinary materials. But home, when we find it, is never ordinary. It is the mystery at the heart of every human project. It is the receding object, occasionally glimpsed, sometimes even caught up with but never finally corraled. Our journeys toward it corkscrew and burrow. They head forward and back. They take us through tunnels of solace, leave us foundering in deep woods, lose us in the aisles of a discount store. They expel us onto sunlit plains or the shores of a vast sea. *Where are we?* we think. *Who dealt this mess?*

In one view, the young woman who stepped onto the tracks near my house simply elected to cut it all short and head straight for home. But I think she may have misjudged how fast the engine was coming her way. Perhaps only moments before, she had lifted her forelegs and raked the sky. Perhaps she whinnied and wheeled. I imagine her looking toward the horizon for a clue to how long it was exactly, how many universes away, before she must become a human child, dress in the night, and prepare to board.

ACKNOWLEDGMENTS

I am indebted to A. N. Wilson's biography of Tolstoy, which helped me to imagine the author's final days. For more about the sociological ideas discussed on page 236, readers may consult "The Homeless Mind—Modernization and Consciousness," by Peter Berger, Brigitte Berger, and Hansfried Kellner. I am grateful to Laura Searls for her research on the life of Niels Hansen. Further information appears in the South Dakota Historical Collections, which, since my days in Cambridge, have proved an invaluable resource. A special thanks to Colleen Natalie-Lees for last-minute fact checking and for an ongoing dialogue that has nourished my ties to home. Others I wish to thank are walking around in this book under aliases and will know who they are. Above all, I am grateful to my husband, Andrew Nixon, a refuge as sustaining as any prairie.